Trussville
ALABAMA

A BRIEF HISTORY

Gary Lloyd

THE History PRESS

Published by The History Press
Charleston, SC 29403
www.historypress.net

Front cover, bottom: Slagheap being used as construction material in February 1937 in the area where the Cahaba Village housing project was built, also on land once occupied by an iron furnace. *Alabama Department of Archives and History, Montgomery, Alabama.*

First published 2014

Manufactured in the United States

ISBN 978.1.62619.185.3

Library of Congress CIP data applied for.

Notice: The information in this book is true and complete to the best of our knowledge. It is offered without guarantee on the part of the author or The History Press. The author and The History Press disclaim all liability in connection with the use of this book.

For my wife, Jessica; Mom and Dad; and my brother, David, who have known and supported my dream of having a book published.

CONTENTS

PREFACE

The idea for this work came about in the spring of 2013. I spent most of my weekends in 2013 at the Trussville Public Library, buried in gray boxes of archived materials, maps, photos, old letters and information, sorting it all out and ordering it chronologically. At first, this room felt almost like a jail cell, a tiny room with no outside view. However, once those boxes of archives were opened, the room came alive with the city of Trussville's history, with tales of what life was like before there were various shopping centers in the city, before homes existed on land outside the Cahaba Project. It was a simpler time, with vast green spaces and many outdoor activities near the Cahaba River. I encourage anyone, authoring a book or not, to visit this room in the back corner of the library and learn about Trussville's past, about life in the school halls, in government offices and in the homes of the historic Cahaba Project. You will be glad you visited.

I want to thank the staff at the Trussville Public Library, who got to know me very well during this process. The friendly staff there always answered my questions and provided a great working environment in which to research. I also want to thank Ron Burkett, who assisted me in the photos phase of this project, often spending his time answering questions relating to photo gathering, editing and more.

I especially want to thank my beautiful wife, Jessica, who stuck with me and supported me throughout this long and tedious process, one that ate up most of my weekends during our engagement and the first few months of our marriage. Your encouragement and understanding were key motivators for me to take on this project.

Finally, I want to thank anyone and everyone who has had a hand in developing the city of Trussville's history. Without you, I would have had nothing about which to write. You shaped the city that Trussville is today, a city that more than twenty thousand people call home and a city that is one of the most desired places to call home in Alabama.

GARY LLOYD
Trussville, Alabama
February 15, 2014

INTRODUCTION

Trussville's origins date back nearly two hundred years, settled first by Native Americans and later migrants who came from North Carolina, Tennessee and Kentucky. Like most southern towns, Trussville once was dominated by green areas and farmers who raised crops on fertile land near the Cahaba River, which cuts through Trussville, the longest free-flowing river in the state of Alabama. Trussville experienced industrial growth in the late 1800s as the Reconstruction era moved forward with the addition of a blast furnace in the heart of the community. The Cahaba Project, a homestead made up of nearly three hundred homes built in the late 1930s as part of President Franklin D. Roosevelt's New Deal program that rules Trussville's history and charm, was constructed near the former blast furnace site.

Trussville's government system has existed since the late 1940s, when it incorporated as a town. Former mayors and city councilmen were business leaders in the area, helping to push the city forward. Education has long been a boast in Trussville, leading more families to desire to take up residence within the city's limits. There is no shortage of churches in Trussville, similar to most towns and cities in the heart of the Bible Belt.

The industry and business climate has seemingly grown each year in Trussville as more retail stores and restaurants look for land on which to build in the growing city of more than twenty thousand people.

Trussville has many attractions for its residents and the residents of other nearby northeastern Jefferson County cities. Shopping and dining are the most popular reasons to visit Trussville, but other city landmarks, both natural and man-made, provide a glimpse into a historic past and look forward to a promising future.

Chapter 1

TRUSSVILLE'S INFANCY

The area now home to the city of Trussville has a long and diverse history. The region was claimed, at various times, by Spain, France and England when these countries fought one another for dominance in the New World, until 1783, when the territory became part of the United States at the end of the Revolutionary War.

Modern-day Jefferson County, Alabama, occupies a small northeastern segment of the former Mississippi territory known as Monroe, which formed in 1814. The independent authority of this region belonged to the Indians at this time, and they did not abdicate their control until 1814, when the Creek War of 1813–14 ended. As a result of that war, the Treaty of Fort Jackson ceded about half of Alabama and parts of southern Georgia to the U.S. government.

In 1817, Mississippi was admitted to the Union, and the Alabama territory was created. In 1818, the region that today includes Blount and Jefferson Counties, as well as parts of Etowah and Walker Counties, was designated as Blount County. On December 14, 1819, Alabama was admitted as the twenty-second state to the Union. As Indians ceded land, about 75 percent of the state was open to white settlement between 1814 and 1820.

The first known settler to occupy the Trussville area was Warren Truss, a man of English descent. A farmer by occupation, Truss was born in Pitt County, North Carolina, on May 12, 1772, the son of Samuel and Mary Forbes Truss Sr. Samuel Truss Sr. raised a big family, and three sons—Joel, Warren and Samuel Jr.—are of interest in the history of Trussville and

Alabama. Joel Truss was the first son to leave North Carolina and head west, leaving sometime before 1810 and stopping in Georgia and South Carolina before entering Alabama. Samuel Truss Jr. and Warren Truss left within the next decade or so, presumably at the urging of Joel.

The last Truss deed on record in Pitt County, North Carolina, was signed by Warren Truss on October 2, 1817, so it appears evident that he left for Alabama sometime after this date. Warren Truss next appeared in St. Clair County, Alabama, in 1820, where he had a family of eight men, one woman and seventeen slaves, according to the 1820 census of St. Clair County. The 1810 census of Pitt County, North Carolina, however, shows Warren Truss with four men, four women and six slaves. Warren Truss's children who appear in Alabama and contributed in part to the early development of Trussville and its surrounding area included Enos, John, Wiley, Arthur, Thomas K., Warren Jr., Susanna, Josiah, Samuel and Zilpha.

The area in which Warren Truss first settled is modern-day Springville, located several miles north of Trussville. That region was named after a large spring located near where Joel and Samuel Truss, as well as numerous others, first settled. Within a few months, Warren Truss had decided to look for a home elsewhere, moving several miles southwest to the banks of the Cahaba River, known by the Indians as Ika Uba and Acadian by the British, on which Trussville is located. Warren Truss first purchased land in Jefferson County on August 22–23, 1821. His land ownership in the county covered nearly one thousand acres, apparently making him a wealthy man for the era.

Shortly after Warren Truss arrived in what is now known as Trussville, other families migrated to the area, attracted by its large land area and fresh water from the Cahaba River. Among the first settlers joining the Truss family were the Morrow, Vann, Blythe, Praytor, Frazier, Hickman, Massey, Worthington, Talley, Holly, Dulaney, Franklin, Bass, Stovall, Williams, Townley, Nash and Clayton families. The families lived close together, and most were farmers, a common occupation during this time period.

Warren Truss died on September 16, 1837. By 1850, North Carolinians ranked second to native Alabamians in regard to origin in the Truss settlement. The Irish immigrants and their descendants were the most represented foreign group in Jefferson County and had a few settlers in Truss. Two-thirds of the Truss beat—or precinct—were landowners in 1850. That number rose to about 70 percent in 1860. Also in 1860, the Eastern District had thirty-three people who owned $5,000 or more in personal property, about half of whom resided in Truss. Truss included two residents who owned $25,000 or more.

The grave site of Warren Truss, Trussville's earliest-known settler, is located at the Trussville Cemetery. *Gary Lloyd.*

The Eastern District included several small slaveholders because the terrain was not too favorable for extensive slave ownership. By 1850, the average number of slaves owned by each slaveholder in Truss was 7, slightly below the 8.4 average in Jefferson County. Jefferson County averaged 9 slaves per owner in 1860. These slaves were generally used to till land and supply labor. Crops raised included wheat, oats, corn, tobacco, cotton and vegetables.

Also by 1850, a wider array of occupational options had developed in Truss and the surrounding areas, including blacksmith, miller, physician, clerk, merchant, clergyman and teacher. In 1850, Truss had two blacksmiths, James L. Glenn and Devirix Clopton, who resided with Warren Truss's widow, Nancy Truss. John C. McKenzie, a merchant, and Enos D. Truss, a clerk apparently serving under McKenzie, also lived with Nancy Truss. The earliest known physician in Truss was Dr. John Spearman Edwards, who settled there sometime in the 1830s. Dr. Zachariah Hagood, who lived and practiced at Hagood's Crossroads, is believed to have served the settlement at an earlier time, since his name is included among many old records in Truss. Israel S. Edens was the community's physician in 1850, and Dr. Francis M. Marshall, upon graduation from the University of Louisiana in 1852, served until 1860 when he moved to Hagood's Crossroads.

Micajah Taylor was one of the first millers, serving in 1850, about thirty years after mills began on the Cahaba River near the present city of Trussville. John Killough was listed in the 1850 census as being a

Cumberland Presbyterian clergyman, likely one of the first ministers of that religion to serve in Truss, since the Cumberland Presbyterian Church was not established as a separate entity until 1867.

In 1850, Truss totaled 549 people. The population had decreased to 530 by 1860; the decrease was caused by just one family.

Dr. Elias Davis served as physician in 1860, although others served in the same capacity during this time. Dr. Bagsdale served between 1864 and 1870, and Dr. J.B. Vann served for about six months in 1860 before moving to Elyton.

Robert H. Glenn was the first recorded mechanic to serve the community, and C.M. Foust was a blacksmith in 1860. Pleasant Martin and M.A. Worthington were listed as merchants in the 1860 census.

It is believed that Truss became known as Trussville in the 1870s. The community was growing, with vast land, a fresh water source in the Cahaba River and sustainable crops. The American Civil War, however, fought between 1861 and 1865, had a significant impact on the community.

Chapter 2

THE CIVIL WAR IMPACTS TRUSSVILLE

Before the Civil War broke out, Trussville was one of the most prosperous agricultural communities in the northern half of the state of Alabama. Almost all able-bodied men in Trussville volunteered for the Confederacy, leaving behind only women, children and men who were too paltry for service or possessed occupations of necessity in the community. The men who volunteered brought with them just about every mule and horse and food stored for the next year. The land in Trussville was virtually deserted except for small gardens and sections of farmland that those who stayed behind cultivated.

The only men in Trussville considered unfit for service because of old age who remained behind were Hugh, Morrow and Elijah Sims. Others who remained behind for at least a portion of the Civil War years were M.K. Vann, S.T. Vann, J. Carlisle, B. Praytor, T. Franklin, J. Truss, R.J. Vann, J.B. Vann and A.B. Tucker.

The Confederate government took 10 percent of all meat, corn and wheat in storage or that was being raised for support of its army and navy. The tenth taken was designated as a war tax, known as a "tax in kind." Felix M. Wood was the receiver of the tax in Trussville. Set aside for government use, the confiscated provisions were amassed in a stone storehouse that had been converted into a warehouse for these supplies. The warehouse, which belonged to Captain Thomas K. Truss and Marcus Worthington, was well filled with supplies when, on April 20, 1865, General James H. Wilson and a brigade of Federal soldiers came

Thomas K. Truss's grave site is located at the Trussville Cemetery. Truss organized "Truss's Home Guards" during the Civil War. *Gary Lloyd.*

through. The Federals took all they could and attempted to burn the storehouse, which was located on Georgia Road and Jasper-Talladega Road, now the corner of Main Street and North Chalkville Road. The stench of burning wheat was stifling, though most was salvaged and ground into flour.

The Federal troops burned other houses, drove away cattle and sheep and took with them serviceable horses and mules. One of the burned buildings was a combination store and post office owned by Thomas K. Truss, a building that had stood where Glenn's Store was eventually located. To prevent such a raid on Trussville, Thomas K. Truss had organized "Truss's Home Guards." A detachment of Wilson's raiders who burned the storehouse was under the command of John T. Croxton, brigadier general of U.S. Volunteers.

The raid in Trussville was one of many by General Wilson and his troops in March and April 1865, destroying most of the state of Alabama's arms-manufacturing abilities and rendering the Confederacy's natural resource base relatively useless. Wilson's raid is considered the largest cavalry raid in the American Civil War, though it had little effect on the war's outcome. The Confederacy was already waning, as General Robert E. Lee surrendered to Union general Ulysses S. Grant in Virginia on April 9, 1865. For the raid across Alabama, Wilson organized and trained more than thirteen thousand troops in northeast Alabama for several months before launching the raid on March 22, 1865.

The Union defeated the Confederacy, ending the four-year war in 1865, abolishing slavery and preserving the union of the states. Trussville suffered quite a blow at the close of the Civil War, losing materials in the storehouse raid and crops in its farmland. As debilitating as the Civil War era was for Trussville and the nation, the Reconstruction era turned it around, and quickly.

Chapter 3

TRUSSVILLE TAKES SHAPE

Following the Civil War, Trussville picked back up on its prewar prosperity and growth.

In 1869, the Trussville Academy, the area's first educational institution, was formed by Professor R.G. Hewitt. The 1870 census showed Hewitt, G.T. Morrow and M. Montgomery registered as "teaching school," the first recorded census tabulation listing any teachers in Trussville. The first school building was a one-room log cabin structure located between present-day U.S. Highway 11 and the Alabama Great Southern Railroad tracks. The sixty- by forty-foot room accommodated one hundred students of elementary and high school age, the average being about eleven years old.

Churches were built bigger in Trussville in this time period after the Civil War. The most significant addition to Trussville by 1870 during the Reconstruction era, however, was the railroad, which reached Trussville in 1870. The Alabama and Chattanooga Railroad Company completed its 295-mile project from Chattanooga, Tennessee, to Meridian, Mississippi, in 1870–71. The railroad addition to Trussville meant more jobs for local residents.

The trains that passed through brought regular mail, freight shipments and passengers from the eastern United States. It also meant more industry in the 1880s. On December 21, 1886, the Birmingham Furnace and Manufacturing Company was incorporated by a group of men from Uniontown, Pennsylvania. The first land company was the Trussville and Cahaba River Land Company, which incorporated on March 19, 1887. That same year, a tract of land was purchased from the Trussville and Cahaba

River Land Company, and construction of a furnace began. A large portion of the furnace built that year came from material from the dismantled Lemont Furnace in Fayette County, Pennsylvania. The furnace was located on the land where the historic school on Parkway Drive is now located. The finished stack, sixty-five feet high and seventeen and a half feet in the wash, was blown in at noon on April 8, 1889. Prior to the sale, the Louisville and Nashville Railroad built a line of tracks to serve the furnace's needs. A special train left the union depot in Birmingham at 10:15 a.m. to celebrate the opening of the furnace. Among the prominent individuals on board were Superintendent William Newhold, Assistant Superintendent B.F. Dickson, Louisville and Nashville Railroad general ticket agent C.B. Compton, Birmingham Furnace and Manufacturing Company secretary and treasurer R.D. Smith and many others. On April 13, 1889, it was reported that the furnace was turning out good-quality iron, and the company's officers were very pleased with the results. The furnace remained in blast until the middle of 1893, when it was blown out due to the diminishing demand for pig iron.

In late 1896, the furnace was put back in blast under the Trussville Furnace Company but operated only a few months before being blown out again. The main difficulty of the furnace was the high cost of raw material transportation. Red hematite was mined within a few miles of the furnace but not in sufficient quantity to satisfy the operation's needs. Additional ore was brought from the Birmingham and Bessemer districts to supplement the local supply; brown hematite was brought from Bartow and Oremont, Georgia; and coke was secured from Birmingham.

The Trussville Furnace, Mining and Manufacturing Company took over the furnace property on September 1, 1899. The incorporators were local men Henry W. Perry, Tunstall B. Perry and Robert D. Smith. It was not put in blast until 1901 and operated only a few months. On July 10, 1902, the furnace property was purchased by the Lacey Buek Iron Company. The furnace was rebuilt and beehive coke ovens were introduced. The stalk was expanded to eighty feet, and the wash was widened to twenty-two and a half feet. It was blown in during 1903 and christened the "Ella." The furnace operated under this company until it was acquired on July 1, 1906, by the Southern Steel Company, which rebuilt the furnace but did not enlarge it. By this time, it was rated at seventy-two thousand tons annually, up from seventy thousand under Lacey Buek Iron Company, and there were 212 workmen's houses attached to the plant. In 1907, the Southern Steel Company bankrupted. The Southern Iron and Steel Company acquired the furnace in 1909, but it was blown out in 1910.

This company defaulted on its bonds in 1911, and the furnace was passed to the Michigan Trust Company.

The furnace remained idle between 1910 and 1917, when the Birmingham Trussville Iron Company was organized, taking control of the furnace. The furnace was blown in for the final time in the spring of 1918, operating until the spring of 1919. The furnace remained abandoned until its dismantling in 1933.

Dyer N. Talley was one of the most active businessmen in Trussville from 1880 to 1928. He built a general merchandise store in 1880. In 1890, a two-story brick building was constructed for his store, at the time the largest building in Trussville. Talley joined the Confederate army in 1861 and served all four years of the Civil War, never sustaining a battle wound.

One of Trussville's valuable productions was sandstone, taken from a quarry that runs alongside present-day Green Drive. In 1928, it was one of the main industries in Trussville, as sandstone could be shipped to many cities and sections of the Southeast.

The industrial center Trussville had become and the influx of a great consuming population during the Roaring Twenties converted a once cotton and grain region into a very prosperous dairy and trucking area. By 1928, Trussville had one main street along which all of its businesses were located, with homes scattered in every direction. Between U.S. Highway 11 and the railroad tracks was a wooded tract of several acres, used as a playground by children and for sports. The nearby Little Cahaba River provided swimming, bathing and fishing opportunities. Trussville had iron ore, coal, limestone, sandstone, timber soil, water, transportation, schooling, churches and opportunity. In 1928, businessmen and farmers alike said Trussville had "everything here that [it] needed to make a big city," according to a December 30, 1928 article in the *Birmingham News–Age Herald.*

Chapter 4

A NEW DEAL FOR TRUSSVILLE

The stock market crash of October 29, 1929, and the ensuing Great Depression sent shockwaves throughout the United States and the world. The Great Depression devastatingly affected rich and poor countries, cities and people. The presidential election of 1932 between Republican incumbent Herbert Hoover and Democratic nominee Franklin D. Roosevelt of New York was the beginning of change for the nation, as well as for Trussville. Roosevelt won the election largely due to his optimistic personality.

Roosevelt's New Deal was a series of economic programs enacted between 1933 and 1936, focusing on relief, recovery and reform as part of progressing from the Great Depression. The programs centered on relief for the unemployed and poor, recovery of the economy and reform of the financial system to prevent another depression.

The property on which the blast furnace was located in Trussville was sold in 1935 to Birmingham Homestead Incorporated, a Federal Housing Administration project. In the time the furnace was idle, the site served as a prison camp, called Jefferson County Camp No. 3. It accommodated between forty-five and seventy-five prisoners, who were primarily involved in roadwork in the county. All the prisoners were white, and the average prison term was just more than two years. Five apartments for prison guards were provided, and a blacksmith shop and barn were also parts of the prison. The prison camp was demolished in preparation for the Federal Housing Administration's project.

During the Great Depression years, the federal government attempted to relieve many citizens in the low-income bracket. The idea of developing homesteads with a moderate amount of acreage was considered and later pursued throughout the United States. In Jefferson County, a committee of prominent local citizens, including Robert Jemison Jr., Charles F. DeBardeleben and J.F. Lies, selected a site in Trussville in plain view of the slagheap from the dismantled furnace, giving the homestead project the name "Slagheap Village," later to be known as "Cahaba Village" and "the Project."

Senator John H. Bankhead and Dr. M.L. Wilson accompanied the trio on its inspection trip to Trussville, where it became apparent that the property would not be suitable for a homestead development. Resettlement administrator Dr. Rexwell Tugwell came to the area on an inspection trip. The area contained thirty houses for white and forty houses for black occupants, some of these being the former workmen's houses connected to the furnace. Tugwell and his associates decided to provide homes in the area for neither the homestead operation nor victims of the Great Depression but instead for a quality suburban residential development. "Slagheap Village" was later called "Cahaba Village," after the nearby Cahaba River. Prior to the land's being purchased and the homes constructed, though, the residing families had to be relocated. The black families were moved to a project site called the Forties, an area still in Trussville today, perched atop Valley Road near the Tiffany Estates subdivision. Most of the white families relocated to the Roper Hill area.

At Tugwell's suggestion, W.H. Kestler drew up the layout plans for the project, and he was thereafter called the "town planner." Cahaba Project consisted of 287 residential units—243 homes and 44 duplex unites—constructed from 1936 to 1938 at an overall cost of $2,661,981.26. The total cost included work on public utilities, streets, curbs, gutters and public buildings, including the high school, community building and cooperative store. The acreage cost was not included. Skirting the housing development was a green stretch of properties designated as park areas to protect the encroachment of any development that may detract from the beauty of the community.

The properties took two years to construct and were opened in April 1938. A waterworks, sewage disposal plant, paved and lighted streets and some sidewalks were provided.

The residents of Cahaba met in June 1938 for the purpose of organizing the "Cahaba Association." Nominations were made for the association's

The intersection of Park Place, Magnolia Street and Parkway Drive in the Cahaba Project. *Gary Lloyd.*

president, vice-president and secretary-treasurer. Those elected to the positions were Mrs. R.G. Ussery, Mrs. James Baskerville and Mr. W.E. Lamons, respectively.

At the August 25, 1938 meeting of the Cahaba Association, a report on telephones was made. According to the minutes, 80 percent of the village's residents had been contacted, and 50 percent of them had signed for phones.

New officers were elected for the following term at the October 6, 1938 meeting. W.D. Miller was elected president, Mrs. J.E. Baskerville was named vice-president, Mrs. Ross Ellenburg was named secretary and Grady Borland was elected treasurer. The association consisted of several committees, including the executive, constitution, sidewalk, telephone, greetings, beautification, recreation, social activities, water, program, history, publicity, transportation, safety and fire equipment. At the August 1939 meeting, it was announced that there were thirty new residents of the village.

At the October 1939 meeting, new officers for the upcoming year were elected. H.T. Rogers was elected president, Paul Krebs was named vice-president, Mrs. Dick Shadoin was named secretary and Roland Carreker was elected treasurer. Rogers totaled sixty-five votes for president, while incumbent W.D. Miller gained fifty-nine. The August 12, 1940 minutes show that 233 residents were surveyed about bus service to and from Birmingham. The residents overwhelmingly favored it, with 227 voting in favor of bus service to just 6 who were not in favor.

At the October 1940 association meeting, Ray A. Hodge was elected the next president, Mrs. Guy Ussery was named vice-president, Mrs. Harry N. Ross was elected secretary and Miles Carter was elected treasurer.

At its June 9, 1941 meeting, the association reported that the Works Progress Administration, the New Deal's largest agency, would fund a park leader to supervise the children when playing in the village's park. The supervisor was to be in the park five days a week, six hours per day. The community was to furnish playground equipment for about thirty-three dollars.

Hodge was reelected as president of the newly named Cahaba Community Association in October 1941. Aubrey Awry was elected vice-president, Mrs. R.S. Terry was elected secretary and J.T. Plonk was named the treasurer. John Waters took Plonk's place in January 1942 when Plonk resigned.

Each resident of Cahaba was asked in February 1942 to have a garden. It was reported in the February 9, 1942 association minutes that a book on gardens was available for twenty-five cents, and copies would be available in the community's cooperative store.

Ben Irby was elected the Cahaba Community Association's president in October 1942. Noah Norman was elected vice-president, John Waters was named treasurer and Joe Norman was elected secretary. The executive board consisted of Guy Ussery, Milton Bates, Fred Powell, Leon Reese and Sam Davis.

The new community manager, A.C. Hester, was introduced at the November 9, 1942 association meeting. He explained the transfer of the Project from the Farm Security Administration to the Federal Public Housing Authority, family selection and family transfers. A.C. Hester stated the following:

> *No transfer to a larger house unless there has been an increase in the family.*
> *A man and wife alone can't have a house larger than a four-room house.*
> *A man and wife with one child would be eligible for a five-room house.*

A.C. Hester said at the meeting that there was nothing in sight for the sale of the houses for the duration and that there would be no painting or major improvements before June 30, 1943. He said that the government would not demand the new occupant of the house to purchase improvements from the old occupant.

The 1943 election of Cahaba Community Association officers was held on October 11, 1943. V. Garnett Kee Jr. was elected president, Mrs. H.H.

Southerland was named vice-president, Mrs. G.B. Howey was elected secretary and H.T. Rogers was elected treasurer. The executive committee consisted of Evans Bagley, William Ennis, George Grogan, Jack Thornton and Emmett Wilcox.

At the March 9, 1944 meeting, A.C. Hester explained the plan of the Federal Public Housing Authority to defederalize the handling of the project by June 30. The Cahaba Community Association stated that it was possible for the community to purchase inventory at cost from the housing authority and be debt free of the government. A.C. Hester suggested the board and some other Cahaba Community Association members form a committee to consider this seriously and meet with the housing authority to work out the plan of carrying out the suggestion. The election of officers for 1944 was held on November 6, 1944. Henry Rodgers bested Garnett Kee and Bill Miller for association president. Jack O'Neill was elected vice-president, R.A. Petree was named treasurer and M.S. Buck was elected secretary. The executive committee was composed of Mrs. Joe Jasper, Mrs. T.C. Wells, Wm. Natter, Grady Lancaster and A.V. Wilkins.

Paul Krebs was elected the Cahaba Community Association president on October 9, 1945. Bill Miller was elected vice-president, Mrs. T.C. Wells was elected secretary and Roland Long was named treasurer. In a letter dated July 15, 1946, it was stated that the Cahaba Project would be disposed of on or before April 1, 1947. "The plan for distribution is in progress of formulation, but none of the details of the plan have been announced by Washington," the letter states.

According to the letter, it was the government's policy to give every residential tenant, provided the tenant met eligibility requirements for homestead occupancy at the time of admission, the first opportunity to purchase his dwelling. The prices reflected normal market value, but a substantial down payment would be required. In an August 17, 1946 letter from Paul Krebs to A.C. Hester, Krebs stated that the people of the Cahaba Project were recently asked through the local newspaper, the *Cahaba Hub*, to express their feelings about the possibility of becoming an incorporated town. The answers showed a strong sentiment favoring incorporation, according to Krebs.

Paul Krebs wrote that the paramount problem of the projected sale of the homes was the proper disposition of the public utilities serving the community. The community, Krebs wrote, would be confronted with the problem of maintaining such services as street lighting, sewers, streets, garbage collection and more. "It is therefore the feeling of the committee that the Cahaba Community should be incorporated; and we would appreciate your opinion in this matter inasmuch as the Government is the sole property owner," wrote Krebs.

Krebs concluded his letter by asking Hester whether he would give consideration to the financial soundness of the utilities if the people of Cahaba were given the opportunity to purchase them. He also asked A.C. Hester to make any revisions to the incorporation before the sale. At the August 22, 1946 Cahaba Community Association meeting, pros and cons of the incorporation of Cahaba alone was discussed, as well as the possibility of including Trussville. It was suggested that the people of Trussville advise the government that they desired to be included in the corporate limits. A motion was passed unanimously that Paul Krebs appoint three additional members to serve with W.W. Marshall and Miller for the purpose of forming a plan of incorporation and operation of a city government to serve both Cahaba and Trussville. Krebs appointed Alton Williams, Jack Thornton and Richard Beard. All who attended this meeting were requested to contact ten or twelve of their neighbors, explain the proposed plan and report back at an executive committee meeting on August 30, 1946.

At that meeting, feedback was given. According to the meeting's minutes, Dewey Gabert reported sixteen out of sixteen contacts favoring incorporation. Dewey Miller reported twelve of twelve favoring, Arthur Dowsing reported nine of nine favoring and Art Collings reported ten out of eleven favoring. Tate reported his contacts were in favor, Miller reported nine favoring and Paul Krebs reported that eight were in favor. Beard said that forty-five of fifty Trussville residents were in favor and that five of nine Roper Hill residents favored incorporation.

Marshall, Thornton, Williams and Miller were named representatives from the community to serve with four others from Trussville. Beard was named a representative of both the Cahaba Project community and Trussville to draw up plans and details to be submitted to the people of both sections. Beard reported at the October 8, 1946 Cahaba Community Association meeting that a volunteer fire department had been organized and that plans were in progress to buy a fire truck. Washington did not approve the fire truck, but when three houses were destroyed by fire and a fourth scorched when a kerosene stove caught on fire, the community was proven right in its request for a fire truck. The Trussville Business Men's Club, Civitan Club and others worked together to attempt to obtain a modern fire truck.

Willis Marshall and William Miller reported that they had contacted the government regarding incorporation in the event of the sale of the houses so the community could buy the utilities and public improvements. At the same meeting, Alton Williams was elected president of the association for 1946–47. John Yarbrough was elected vice-president, Rowland Long became treasurer and Mrs. Claude Parkell was elected secretary. Elected as board members were Paul Krebs, Dewey Gabert, W.W. Marshall, Hosmer Roberson, Richard Beard and Dewey Miller.

According to the October 8, 1946 annual report of the Liaison Committee of the Cahaba Community Association, there was a joint committee meeting on September 24, 1946, between Cahaba and Trussville representatives. It was unanimously agreed that the incorporated municipality should include both Cahaba and Trussville. A.C. Hester, the community manager, stated at this meeting that he had advised the Cahaba Executive Committee that the government would defray the expense of incorporating the government property and that he felt certain that the government would be agreeable to extending the corporate limits to include a part of Trussville, provided it was shown that this was the will of the Trussville residents. A Trussville representative, Horace Norell, was then instructed to write to A.C. Hester, requesting that a portion of Trussville be included in the incorporated municipality.

Alton Williams announced at the November 7, 1946 meeting that government representative Arthur Taylor was expected to present a plan soon for selling the water works. With this announcement, three committees were appointed. The Public Utilities, Homestead and Planning Committees were appointed. Paul Krebs was named chairman of the Public Utilities Committee, with Rowland Long and W.W. Marshall also serving. The duty of this committee was to declare a plan for fire protection of the Trussville area surrounding Cahaba and to work with government agents on formulating a plan for selling the utilities.

John Yarbrough was named chairman of the Homestead Committee, with Dewey Miller and Hosmer Roberson also contributing. The committee's duty was to work with Cahaba residents and the government agents to obtain the best possible plan for the sale of the houses. The executive board members composed the Planning Committee, which had the task of working toward the incorporation of the community and becoming an incorporated municipality. At this meeting, Dewey Miller and W.W. Marshall were asked to develop a plan of operations for a city form of government. Dewey Gabert and Alton Williams were asked to present plans for zoning and to work out a building code.

A March 11, 1947 letter from the Federal Public Housing Authority briefly outlined the proposed incorporation of the town of Trussville. The letter stated that the Cahaba Project was a fine example of planning for semi-subsistence homes that would be protected from the uncontrolled growth of its neighbor, Trussville. Two Cahaba Project streets, Chalkville Road and Parkway Drive, connected with Trussville, and all border lots in the Cahaba Project were arranged so that they faced away from Trussville. All minor streets had been planned so that their connections with Trussville were made by way of Chalkville Road or Parkway Drive.

"The time has come now to join these separate communities as an Incorporated Town," the letter stated. "In order to do so there must be more direct connections between the two communities and a pooling of their interests so that a well organized community will be attained."

The letter addressed one community need: an adequate business area. The business center in Trussville at the time, along the state highway, was thought to be able to serve the future town of Trussville and the surrounding county farm area adequately. The letter stated that the area needed revisions, such as street widening by setback and a focal point where a city hall building, post office, fire department and town bank could be constructed. It was recommended that a portion of a block made by creating a new street parallel to Chalkville Road be acquired for that purpose. The area that fit best was located near the grade school along Chalkville Road. With certain revisions of streets, the fire department could reach connecting streets for the whole town.

The Federal Public Housing Authority continued to say in the letter that Trussville limit, through zoning, the use of land along the state highway for business use. This was recommended for several reasons, including the protection of the property owners whose homes were along the highway, the safety and protection of pedestrians and because a concentrated business center could be operated more efficiently than a business area in a ribbon-like development. The housing authority recommended that setback lines be established so that the highway would be one hundred feet in width with additional setbacks required for service stations. Three connections with Trussville were proposed by the State Highway Commission, with the goal of access being controlled and safety for pedestrians assured.

The letter recommended that both sides of the Cahaba River be dedicated as parklands, as well as the Mall, a large grassy area in the Cahaba Project, and triangular area near present-day Brentwood Avenue. The grassy area between Magnolia Court and Hewitt Street was also recommended to be kept as parkland and also as parking for the nearby church.

The letter went on to say that the housing authority was fully aware of Trussville's process of incorporation. The letter acknowledged that Trussville proposed to incorporate as a town according to the law, setting up a mayor and commission and then revising the setup to have a city or town manager type of government.

At the April 8, 1947 Cahaba Community Association meeting, Henry Rogers, chairman of the Survey Committee, explained the work his committee had done toward the purchase of the Cahaba homes. He explained the terms of fourteen loan companies that answered a questionnaire sent to them by his committee, concerning their terms of obtaining various types of loans. Charts containing all interest rates and fees based on a $4,000 loan were handed out to all association members. Rogers assured the association that by cooperating, the community could greatly reduce the cost of handling the loans. Beard said at the meeting that the plans for incorporation of the community were complete, including a government signature. A.C. Hester reported that the Federal Public Housing Authority was working earnestly toward the sale of the homes and that the authority wanted Cahaba residents to obtain the best possible loans with the best interest rates. A.C. Hester said that no prices would be set and no homes sold until June 1, 1947. He explained that alleys and green belts would be added to lots adjoining and that parks and vacant lots would be dedicated to the municipality by the government.

In a May 1, 1947 letter from Rowland Long, Horace Norrell and Alton Williams to Arthur Taylor, who was assistant director for real estate and disposition for the Federal Public Housing Authority, plots of land that the community wanted dedicated to the city of Trussville upon incorporation were listed. "We have observed the growth of communities such as ours and have noticed the many times that the city fathers have erred in not allocating sufficient space for parks and playgrounds," the letter stated. "We anticipate a healthy growth in this community and hope to avoid some of these mistakes by giving much forethought and long range planning."

The letter stated also that the community leaders realized that there were many undeveloped tracts and vacant lots suitable for home sites. It was not the city's desire to request such tracts for park areas except in cases in which it was of extreme importance. The letter asked the Federal Public Housing Authority that fourteen government-owned tracts be designated to Trussville when the community became an incorporated town. The tracts included what is now the Mall area, areas surrounding the Cahaba River, areas around the Alabama Great Southern Railroad and U.S. Highway 11 and a portion of a tract that was dedicated to the Jefferson County Board of Education for a football stadium that included classrooms and athletic fields.

In a May 26, 1947 letter from Arthur Taylor to Alton Williams, Taylor explained that the Federal Public Housing Authority was under a mandate from Congress to dispose of all subsistence homestead project properties quickly. Taylor wrote that it was the housing authority's intention to commence the sale of the project homes within thirty to forty-five days, depending on work to be done in drafting contracts. Taylor said in the letter that the housing authority had hoped that the sale of the homes would commence after the town was incorporated and had acquired the utility systems. Taylor wrote:

> *In this manner, the unit purchasers would know definitely that they would continue to have water and sewerage services and would have some definite idea of the monthly costs for such services. While we feel that the best interests of the project occupants will be served by selling the systems to an incorporated Township, if such incorporation does not take place we will sell the systems to the highest bidder. This may result in the project* [sic] *occupants having to pay more for water and sewerage services than would be the case if these utilities were sold to an incorporated Township.*

At the May 28, 1947 Cahaba Community Association meeting, letters from the government were read, confirming that the homes would be sold to the individuals of Cahaba and not a realty company. It was reported that the Federal Public Housing Authority would not finance the home loans unless the water system was owned and operated by the township. Paul Krebs stated that with 300 to 385 customers necessary, extensions of the water system and sewerage could be made to the Trussville area surrounding Cahaba.

On June 2, 1947, an election was held to determine whether to incorporate the town of Trussville into a city form of government. The election carried, and all property owned by the Federal Public Housing Authority with four legal voters per forty acres of land was included in the area to be incorporated. Cahaba Project was absorbed into the town of Trussville when it was incorporated on June 10, 1947.

Arthur Taylor wrote Alton Williams a letter on July 10, 1947, with good news regarding the purchase of the water and sewerage disposal systems for the community's offered sum of $50,000 in cash. Taylor wrote that upon receipt of an official offer with signatures of proper municipal officials, the housing authority would have an official acceptance of the offer within one week. By July 21, 1947, an election of a mayor and five aldermen was held. Horace Norell was elected mayor, and Mary Lou

Farley, George A. Glenn, Alton Williams, John Yarbrough and Richard Beard were elected aldermen.

The homes and duplexes in the Cahaba Project were sold to individuals in 1947 at prices ranging from $4,400 to $9,000 each. Most homes in the Cahaba Project today cost between $200,000 and $320,000 because of the area's historic value and its proximity to parks, schools, recreation and shopping opportunities.

Chapter 5

GOVERNMENT

On June 10, 1947, the Trussville area was incorporated as a town. The population at the time was 1,443 people. A month later, Horace Norrell was elected as the town's first mayor. A graduate of Phillips High School, Horace Norrell was the owner of Norrell's Super Store in Trussville, and a member of the Georgiana Davis Masonic Lodge and Trussville Methodist Church. Horace Norrell, a charter member of the Trussville Civitan Club, was married to the former Mabel Glenn, a lifetime Trussville resident. Horace Norrell was Trussville's mayor through 1960.

The town's first clerk was A.V. Hoover, though Mary Louise Hill served as acting town clerk for a brief period. The town's attorney was Judge Needham A. Graham. The initial police force was composed of just two men, police chief Joe B. Vann and patrolman A.E. Quick. Winn Strickland was the town's second clerk, serving until 1963. The mayor and five aldermen served in Trussville's city hall building, built in 1945, on Main Street. The city's jail was located behind the building. The city's second city hall building was built in 1949 on South Chalkville Road and was leased to the town for one hundred dollars per month.

On January 15, 1948, the U.S. government dedicated and deeded all of the parks property to the town. The formal transfer of the deed occurred on February 18, 1948. In December 1950, the waterworks and gas board of the town of Trussville, a municipal corporation, was established. The name was later changed in July 1955 to the Utilities Board of the town of

Trussville. The town purchased the cooperative store, a large brick building on Parkway Drive in the Cahaba Project, in 1951.

On May 31, 1957, the town officially became a city, with a population of 2,161 people. In 1958, a gas peak shaving plant was built at a cost of $200,000. On November 1, 1947, the town purchased the sanitary sewage treatment plant from the government, along with the waterworks. A sewage-pumping station had also been erected as a booster station to the sewage treatment plant.

The current Trussville Municipal Building on Main Street was erected by the city of Trussville and the Utilities Board in 1959. The city staff moved into the building on July 1, 1959. Charles H. McCauley was the architect, and Hare Construction Company was the builder. The building covered 15,012 square feet of floor space and was built and furnished at about $225,000, paid for by water and gas utilities. The city occupied about one-third of the space, with the rest occupied by the Utilities Board, volunteer fire department and police department. The auditorium had a seating capacity of 150 people. The jail was located in the right wing of the building and had seven cells—five for men and two for women. The building was dedicated on August 21, 1960. The building was renovated and expanded in August 1993 and still serves as the location for city business, the police department and Trussville City Council meetings.

The Trussville Municipal Building is the location of Trussville City Council meetings, as well as all city business. *Gary Lloyd.*

James W. Barr was elected as Trussville's second mayor, serving from 1960 to 1964. Barr, an Ensley High School graduate, was a Trussville city councilman prior to his election and had lived in Trussville since 1948. He had served as an air force officer during World War II. At the time of Barr's election in 1960, the city's population had grown to 2,510 people.

John Yarbrough, the former city councilman, was elected mayor in 1964 and served through 1968. Living in Trussville since 1938, John Yarbrough had headed up the police and street departments. He was a past president of the Trussville Civitan club and was married to the former Pearl Wilson. John Yarbrough was an executive with Yielding's Department Store.

Roland Crabbe was the city of Trussville's fourth mayor, holding the position from 1968 to 1972. The 1970 census reported that Trussville's population was steadily increasing, up to 2,984 people. Alton Williams was mayor from 1972 to 1976, and Ormond Bentley served in the position as the sixth mayor of the city from 1976 to 1980, defeating incumbent Williams 708 votes to 486 votes in the 1976 election. Roland Crabbe took over for Ormond Bentley in 1980, when Bentley went back to being a city councilman, and served until 1982. Roland Crabbe, fifty-eight, died of a heart attack at a July 1982 Trussville City Council meeting. He had been president of the Jefferson County Mayors' Association and head of the Alabama League of Municipalities executive committee.

David Nicodemus was the city's mayor from 1982 to 1984. Originally from West Virginia, he moved to Trussville in 1971 as a key member of four executives who founded Amerex Corporation, a fire extinguisher and safety system manufacturer. David Nicodemus also served as a city councilman and Utilities Board member.

Charles Grover was elected to the mayor position in 1984. Grover, a Trussville resident since 1954, was a veteran of World War II and the Korean War. Prior to running for alderman in 1964, he was a worker at Jefferson County United Appeal for fourteen years and was mayor of the Yadkin community in Fort Bragg, North Carolina. He was also employed for fourteen years by the Chicago Bridge and Iron Company. A member of Holy Infant of Prague Catholic Church in Trussville, Charles Grover won a Distinguished Service Award from the Alabama League of Municipalities in 1996 for his twenty years of service as an elected official. Charles Grover had served two terms as a councilman before serving as mayor from 1984 to 1996. Charles Grover died in April 2000. Trussville experienced much of its widest growth residentially and commercially under Charles Grover's leadership. The 1980 census reported 3,200 Trussville residents, but the city

Former Trussville mayor Charles Grover. *Trussville Public Library archives.*

was about to grow significantly. In 1985, the city expanded in all directions during a frenzied period. The City of Birmingham had attempted to annex the high school, which was less than one year old, and more of eastern Jefferson County, prompting Trussville's own plan to annex. From the middle of May 1985 through the year's end, the Trussville City Council held annexation meetings several times per week. Some Trussville residents wanted the city's borders left alone. Charles Grover said at the time that he heard that a lot but that there was no way Trussville could stay the same. He said that Birmingham then would surround Trussville.

In 1985, Trussville annexed land for eighty houses to be built on property owned by Coy Simmons, eighteen to twenty houses to be built on property belonging to Roy Stackhouse on U.S. Highway 11 and new homes and office warehouse buildings to be built on about 80 acres off South Chalkville Road. The city also annexed 1,950 acres of land on what was known as the Deerfoot property.

In May 1986, the Trussville City Council approved Autrey-Cole Development Co. to build almost two hundred homes, an office building and a small shopping center in Trussville over the next few years. The new subdivision was known as Calumet Downs, still a popular Trussville neighborhood that includes family-sized homes and garden homes. The property had been annexed into the city just two months prior to the approval of the development. In June of that same year, the Trussville City Council annexed the Cahaba Valley Golf and Country Club, now known as the Trussville Country Club, extending the city's borders into St. Clair County near present-day Moody.

Then U.S. vice president George H. Bush visited Trussville in July 1986, bringing more notice to the city. Alabama Republican Party executive director Marty Connors said at the time that the Trussville area was the third-fastest growing Republican stronghold in the state of Alabama, based on straight-ticket Republican voting in the 1984 presidential election.

By 1990, the city's population had more than doubled, up to 8,044 people from the 3,200 people recorded at the time of the 1980 census. In August 1992, the Trussville City Council agreed to contribute $250,000 to the Jefferson County Commission to help buy land for what is now known as Watterson Parkway, the overpass that spans the railroad tracks and Pinch Gut Creek. The overpass is a popular link from Main Street to the south side of the city and a way to get to the south side of Trussville if a train is stopped, blocking the South Chalkville Road area. The deal included evicting some businesses from the area, including Trussville Sand and Gravel. The overpass was completed in 1993.

In late 1994, the Trussville City Council adopted the U.S. 11 Corridor Plan, which included zoning recommendations, development guidelines and a transportation plan for U.S. Highway 11 in Trussville. The city had imposed a moratorium on new construction for about one year in the corridor as the plan was drafted. Proponents said at the time that the plan was needed to prevent rapid and uncontrolled growth to the U.S. Highway 11 area. Critics said that the plan imposed too many regulations and would

Gene Melton has been Trussville's mayor since 1996. *Ron Burkett.*

halt development. Charles Grover called the plan a good investment for the city of Trussville.

By March 1995, the city of Trussville was still expanding its borders to create new homes for incoming residents. The Maplewood subdivision, consisting originally of 102 homes, including 37 garden homes, was annexed into Trussville that month. Two months later, the now Colonial Village at Trussville apartment complex, known then as the Meadows of Trussville, was approved. The complex originally included 376 apartments in twenty buildings on twenty-seven acres on the south end of the city. All of the apartment buildings were to be completed by July 1996.

Gene Melton, a Trussville city councilman, was elected as the city's mayor in 1996, defeating fellow city councilman Gerald Glenn in a runoff. Melton has won each of the four mayoral elections since 1996, and he has been instrumental in the protection of the Cahaba River, the growth in population and business and the promotion of compressed natural gas as an alternative fuel source for city vehicles.

Trussville City Council Members

People who have served as aldermen or councilmen in the city of Trussville include Richard Beard Sr., George A. Glenn, John Yarbrough, Mary Lou Farley, Alton Williams, R.W. McLendon, Henry T. Rogers, Paul D. Bagley, James W. Barr, Richard Beard Jr., John Brock, Sedric Mann, Henry Reeder, Harry Reich, Everette Jones, Gordon Flynn, H.B. Payne, Robert Jones, James Riddle, Ormond Bentley, James Robinson, James Alexander, Jeanette Alexander, Thomas Brewer, Robert Hardy, Whitten Chasteen, Williams Morrison, A.H. Wright, David Nicodemus, Grady Lancaster, Ralph Mitchell, Karen Waldrop, Joe Hocutt, Dorothy Morris, Sally Payne, David Needham, Doug Massey, Calvin Starlin, Dennis Hill, Jerry Spruiell, Jeffrey Bramer, Raymond Coker, John Garrison, Gerald Glenn, Gene Melton, Jane Bailey, John Reeves, Wayne Taylor, Brian Plant, Buddy Aydelette, Buddy Choat, Anthony Montalto, Perry Cook and Alan Taylor.

The Trussville Post Office

In the early 1830s, the influx of North Carolinians brought the need for more roads so people could travel by horse and horse-drawn wagons. Huntsville Road and Georgia Road were the main thoroughfares, though others were built between settlements to facilitate trade and commerce. Boats were often used on the Cahaba River to transport food supplies, merchandise and home goods from one settlement to another. In Jefferson County's early days, mail was brought once per week by horse from Huntsville and Tuscaloosa. By February 1833, the Truss settlement's size had increased, and there was demand for a post office and for Arthur Truss to serve as postmaster. By 1860, the post office in Truss was among the largest in Jefferson County. The post office was discontinued, however, on October 9, 1866. It was reestablished just a month later, on November 15, 1866. It was discontinued again on August 7, 1868, but was established for good on November 29, 1870. In those first thirty-seven years, postmasters were Arthur Truss, Thomas K. Truss, Hensley S. Thomason, Robert J. Hagood, John C. McKenzie and Joseph Hawkin. From 1870 through 1937, postmasters were John N. Taylor, John P. McDuffie, Dyer Talley, Russell H. Hendon, Mrs. Doll A. Vann, Joel D. Acton, John B. Martin, A.J. Bass Jr., Dyer T. Dew, Martin Dyer Franklin and Paul E. Bradford.

According to an April 22, 1985 letter from the Office of the Postmaster General in Washington, D.C., the post office was originally established as Truss in St. Clair County on March 17, 1828, with John Nash serving as first postmaster. The Jefferson County Post Office in Truss had its name changed to Trussville on November 29, 1870, the day it was reestablished for good.

The Trussville Post Office from the 1930s to 1948 was located in a building near the southwest corner of Main Street. From 1948 to 1958, it was located in the left side of D.N. Talley's store, sharing space with the Pot and Griddle Café. The post office was located in its own building constructed by Sam Liles from 1958 to the spring of 1980. In 1980, the U.S. Post Office opened in Trussville and today remains in its location on Watterson Curve near Main Street.

City Clerks

A.V. Hoover was the town of Trussville's first clerk, and Mary Louise Hill served for a brief period in the summer of 1947. Winn Strickland served from 1947 to 1968, Emile Southerland was city clerk from 1968 to 1981 and Joellen Townsend served in the position from 1981 to 1986. Lynn Porter has been Trussville's city clerk since September 1986.

Trussville Police Department

Joe B. Vann was police chief from 1947 to 1951. Chief Gore and Frank Anderson also served in the position in the early years of Trussville incorporation. Robert Jones was police chief from 1957 to 1964, Carl Stephens led the force from 1964 to 1968, Irving Nash was chief from 1968

Trussville Police Department members in 1960. *Top row, from left*: John Morgan Jr., J.C. Alverson and Lewis Simpson. *Bottom row, from left*: Assistant Chief Carl Stephens, Chief Robert Jones and Sergeant Irving Nash. *Trussville Public Library archives.*

to 1971 and Ernest Hayes was chief from 1972 to 1975. Nash served as police chief again from 1975 to 1997. Don Sivley has been the police chief for the Trussville Police Department since January 1998. Sivley had been an officer with the department since June 1976.

The 1960 police department consisted of six men—Chief Robert Jones, Sergeant Irving Nash, Assistant Chief Carl Stephens, Lewis Simpson, John D. Morgan and J.C. Alverson—tripling its number of police force employees from 1947. Today, the Trussville Police Department consists of sixty-four members: the chief, two lieutenants, eleven sergeants, thirty-six officers, a computer network system administrator, eleven public safety dispatchers and two administrative assistants in the records section. The department is made up of three primary operational areas: administration, patrol and administrative support.

Lieutenant Jeff Bridges heads the administration and investigations division, which consists of the investigations, youth services, training, school officers and jail departments. He took the place of former lieutenant Paul Skaggs, who retired in October 2011. Skaggs had been with the Trussville Police Department since July 1982. In his time there, he'd been a patrolman, evidence technician, investigator, sergeant and lieutenant. His law enforcement career began with the Warrior Police Department in 1979. Lieutenant Eric Rush and Lieutenant Herb Rosenbaum command the patrol division, which is responsible for routine patrol, including crime prevention and detection; enforcement of local criminal and traffic laws; investigating traffic accidents; and rendering aid to citizens. The administrative support division, which consists of communications, records and technical services, is commanded by Lieutenant J.J. Morris.

Trussville Fire and Rescue

The discussion of a fire department began in March 1946, before Trussville was incorporated as a town. A.C. Hester, the Cahaba community manager, said at a Cahaba Community Association meeting that he had made a request to government authorities to have a fire engine transferred from the War Department to Cahaba. Richard Beard headed the volunteer fire department, and the chief was H.W. Suttles. George Glenn was day captain, Joe Hawkins was night captain, Harry Reich was vice-president of the department and Bill Natter was secretary. By October 1946, plans were in place to purchase a fire truck.

Trussville's first and only full-time fire chief, Russell Ledbetter. *Trussville Fire & Rescue.*

Some equipment was inspected that month, but it was determined to not be adequate for a growing community. Hester reported that the government disapproved of the community's request for a fire engine. Upon that news, the Trussville Business Men's Club, Trussville Civitan Club and others began the process of acquiring a modern fire truck.

The chief of the fire department office was established at the August 7, 1947 town meeting. The first fire truck cost $9,000. The fire department remained a volunteer organization with one station until 1998, when Russell Ledbetter was selected from a trio of candidates to lead a department of volunteers and paid firefighters. Ledbetter, at the time a lieutenant with the Bessemer Fire Department and volunteer fire chief with the Palmerdale Fire Department, is still Trussville's fire chief. The city of Trussville includes three fire stations: Station 1 on Main Street, Station 2 on Roper Road and Station 3 on U.S. Highway 11. The department's administration offices and Lewis "Cooter" Simpson Training Facility occupy the former Hewitt Elementary School campus on Cherokee Drive.

Today, there are thirty-four full-time fire department employees, including four administrative staff members. There are eighty-seven volunteers as part of the Trussville Volunteer Fire Department. All of Trussville's full-time firefighters are trained as emergency medical technicians.

Utilities

The water and sewage systems were purchased from the government in 1947 for $50,000, allowing the town of Trussville to own its own water system. Known as Trussville Utilities since 1950, the company serves not only the city of Trussville but also surrounding areas, including Clay and Pinson. As part of Franklin D. Roosevelt's Works Progress Administration program, a well was dug in 1936, and in 1938, a waterworks, sewage system and sewage disposal plant were created. Now with twelve tanks, twelve wells and a filtration plant on Green Drive, Trussville Utilities is one of the larger utilities companies in the area. The Trussville City Council appoints Utilities Board members to serve six-year terms. Chairman Gordon Flynn and Vice-Chairman Don Evans will serve through December 1, 2014. Director Leland Dockery will serve through December 1, 2016, and directors Teddy Gilmer and A.H. Wright will serve through December 1, 2018. In April 2013, Mike Strength, Trussville Utilities's chief financial officer, replaced the retiring Bill Wingate as the company's general manager.

Other Boards, Committees and Departments

Trussville's Beautification Board recommends public beautification projects, evaluates landscape treatments and selects winners for local commercial and residential beautification awards. Each year, the board accepts ballots for its annual Trussville Beautification Awards. The categories for judging are best homeowner maintained, best landscape, best turf, best business, best professionally maintained and best use of color. The awards are presented each May at the Trussville City Fest.

Trussville's Downtown Redevelopment Authority has been in place since December 2010, and its leaders were nominated and approved in March 2011. Jef Freeman is the authority's chairman, Mike Gunter is vice-chairman, Scott Walls is treasurer and Robin Wilkins is secretary. Other members are Eddie Seal, Diane Poole, Joe Howle and David Morgan. The authority is tasked with recruiting proper businesses to occupy downtown Trussville, acquire and lease property and negotiate deals on its own on behalf of the City of Trussville. The main reason the Downtown Redevelopment Authority began meeting in early 2011 centered on America's Thrift Stores signing a fifteen-year lease on a former Food World building on Main Street. The grocery store had closed in September 2010. The Trussville City Council in January 2011 had approved a $28,000 contract with TurnerBatson Architects for planning a downtown revitalization and formalizing the master plan for the downtown district of Trussville. Not wanting a thrift store to occupy a major commercial building on Main Street, the city council in October

2011 approved lending $750,000 to the Downtown Redevelopment Authority to lease the former grocery store. The city also paid $250,000 to end America's Thrift Stores' fifteen-year lease. The City of Trussville has spent about $22,000 per month since October 2011 for rent on the building. The Downtown Redevelopment Authority in July 2013 approved final lease negotiations for two tenants to occupy the former Food World. The tenants are Fresh Value Marketplace, an independent grocer owned by Triple N Enterprises, and 24e Fitness.

The Grow Trussville Committee is an advisory committee tasked with reviewing the business and commercial needs in the city, studying economic trends and cutting-edge ventures, identifying business and commercial enterprises, promoting the city's strengths and recommending policies of establishing an effective, responsible business atmosphere to the Trussville City Council. This committee consists of five Trussville citizens knowledgeable in business and two members of the city council. The committee meets four times per year.

The Trussville Historical Society promotes historic preservation and encourages public interest in the history of the city of Trussville. Venie Payne, who died in February 2013 at the age of ninety-one, served on the original Trussville Historical Society, the Trussville Historical Board, in late 2006 and was instrumental in forming the new Trussville Historical Society in 2007. Payne led the Trussville Historical Board in developing a memorial in Trussville's Civitan Park to honor all veterans of the U.S. Armed Forces.

The city's Industrial Development Board promotes industrial expansion for economic growth and employment. The board is authorized to sell or lease property to industrial tenants to promote this objective. The nine-member board in recent years has been developing and marketing the Trussville Industrial Park on U.S. Highway 11, an area zoned for light industrial development.

Trussville's Inspections Department handles all commercial and residential inspections for the city. All new builders to the city must go over the requirements and renovations to existing buildings, as well as plans for signs, fences, sprinkler systems, pools and accessory structures.

The city's Library Board oversees the operation of the Trussville Public Library and establishes policies.

The municipal court is held at the Trussville Municipal Building on Main Street. The court's jurisdiction covers traffic violations and misdemeanor offenses.

Trussville's Parks and Recreation Board serves in an advisory role, assisting in the development of policies and programs conducted through the Parks and Recreation Department. The department is led by director David Vinson, who has been in that role since 1996, after working for the Birmingham Parks and Recreation Department and as a parks and recreation superintendent in Gadsden. Trussville's parks history really began on January 15, 1948, when the government dedicated and deeded all the parks property to the town. In June 1954, Trussville's community swimming pool, which cost $50,000.00, opened. In 1955, swimming tickets were $0.45 for adults and $0.30 for children under the age of twelve. Season tickets in 1955 were $6.00. The pool that year was under the supervision of Charles Herron. With growing popularity, the rate to swim at the pool increased in 1956, to $0.50 for adults and $0.35 for children. The $6.00 price remained the same in 1957, 1958 and 1960. The Trussville City Pool is still open and popular today, costing $170.00 for a family pass or $100.00 for a single pass. The pool today also features a separate splash park for children age two to twelve. The splash park includes multiple pieces of equipment that spray and pour water.

The John C. Yarbrough Community Center, located beside the Trussville City Pool, was purchased by the town in 1951 with the help of the Federated Women's Clubs of Trussville, who furnished the equipment. In a December 1951 letter from town clerk Winn Strickland to Trussville Parks and Recreation Board chairman J.H. Burgess, Strickland explains some of the town council's expectations, including rental of the center costing ten dollars on weeknights and fifteen dollars on Saturday nights. At an August 20, 1953 meeting, the Parks and Recreation Board established operating rules and regulations for the community center. All activities were to be directly supervised by the recreational director, and everyone using the facility was to be under the director's supervision. Other rules included that a schedule of activities be posted at all times, some activities be restricted to certain age groups, opening and closing times be strictly adhered to, all or part of the building could be rented for private functions if public activities were not scheduled and no one but authorized employees be allowed behind the concession center. Charles Herron was appointed the supervisor of recreation for the town on November 1, 1953. The community center today hosts library book sales and some meetings of civic groups.

The Trussville Sports Complex, the major area for youth sports in Trussville, was completed in 1994. In the first phase of construction, four soccer fields, five baseball fields and one youth football field were built. The complex's four walking and riding trails were also constructed in 1994. Today, the complex is home to two softball fields, nine baseball fields, four

The Trussville Senior Activity Center on Cherokee Drive. *Gary Lloyd.*

soccer fields, a Frisbee disc golf course, one youth football field and the Trussville Racquet Club, which features six clay courts and six hard courts.

The Trussville Parks and Recreation Department also oversees the Trussville Senior Activity Center, which opened its Cherokee Drive location on August 31, 1999. An advisory board for the senior center had been assigned by Mayor Gene Melton, and it included LaRue Meadows, Betty Hocutt, Virginia Lancaster, Catherine Quick, James Perry, Don Solfronk, Everette Jones, David Vinson and Sandi Wilson, who has been the center's director since it opened. The facility consists of a large multipurpose room with two pool tables and many game tables, a private card room, an exercise equipment room, a coffee/television room, a glassed back porch with a fireplace and a multipurpose room with a floating hardwood floor. The center, primarily funded through a community development block grant from the U.S. Department of Housing and Urban Development, once included seniors ages sixty-two and over before the age of participation was lowered to sixty. In 2013, the age of participation was lowered to fifty-five, the first senior activity center in Jefferson County to do so.

In October 2008, a sixty-seven-thousand-square-foot civic center opened on Trussville-Clay Road. Most Trussville Parks and Recreation Department employees are based at the Trussville Civic Center. The facility has about

The Trussville Civic Center on Trussville-Clay Road. *Gary Lloyd.*

sixteen thousand square feet of meeting space and an exhibit hall that can accommodate about one thousand people. The civic center also features a walking track, fitness center and gymnasium. A plaque on the entrance wall honors John LeMaster, chairman of the Trussville Parks and Recreation Board from 1983 to 2005.

Trussville's Planning and Zoning Board is a nine-member board responsible for the compilation and adoption of the city's master plan and subdivision regulations. The board also plays a role in the development of Trussville's zoning ordinances, and it is periodically called on by the city to assist in compiling ordinances pertaining to zoning or land development matters. The board makes recommendations to the Trussville City Council on all zoning matters and annexations and also approves or denies subdivisions or other divisions of property in accordance with established regulations.

Trussville's Public Safety Committee is charged with reviewing concerns from city residents and department heads and making recommendations to the city council regarding these concerns. Concerns include public safety issues, parade permit requests, speed limit changes, stop sign placement and other public safety concerns. The committee is composed of the mayor, a city council member, the police and fire chiefs and four Trussville citizens. The Trussville City Council in July 2013 approved an ordinance that increased the scope of the committee. The ordinance's aim is to increase public participation in disaster preparedness and to provide a forum for residents to share their concerns regarding public safety.

The Trussville Telecommunications Committee considers matters pertaining to cable, telephones and cell towers.

The city's Tree Commission is responsible for establishing street tree plans for major city streets.

The Streets and Sanitations Department is responsible for minor street repairs. Lewis "Cooter" Simpson led this department from 1988 to the summer of 2013, when he retired. Simpson got his start with the city of Trussville in 1957 with the fire department, spent time with the water department from 1958 to 1959 and was a Trussville Police Department patrolman and sergeant/assistant chief from 1959 to 1969. He then spent a number of years with a now closed paper company before returning to the city in 1988 as the head of the Streets and Sanitation Department. His position was filled by Wayne Sullivan, the former director and county engineer of the Jefferson County Roads and Transportation department. The city, as of December 1, 2013, contracted with Advanced Disposal for garbage pickup, recycling and brush pickup.

Chapter 6

EDUCATION

Schooling in Trussville can be traced back to 1869, when Robert Greene Hewitt, a professor from Jefferson County, founded the Trussville Academy. The school building was a one-room log cabin structure located between present-day U.S. Highway 11 and the railroad tracks at South Chalkville Road. As listed in the 1870 census, Hewitt was apparently assisted by G.T. Morrow and M. Montgomery. In 1860, Trussville possessed 28 illiterates to 143 literates, proving it as one of the leading communities in educational achievement for this time period. Many who were educated at the Trussville Academy went on to take prominent positions in the community and surrounding districts. Later, Hewitt donated his property to the community and another larger school was built on the site of present-day Trussville First United Methodist Church. The building served as the community's grammar school from 1903 to 1938, when it became Trussville Methodist Church.

In late 1922, a new school was completed across the street from the grammar school, in the area of the current Trussville City Schools Central Office building. In 1925, it became known as R.G. Hewitt High School, and a total of eleven students formed its first graduating class in 1927. In 1938, the building became Hewitt Elementary School, as a result of a new Hewitt High School being constructed by the government on modern-day Parkway Drive along with the formation of the Cahaba Project. The new high school housed the tenth through twelfth grades. One room on the south side of the building was used as a nursery and

Trussville School students on October 16, 1911. *Kathy Kennedy.*

The 1949 Hewitt football team. *Kathy Kennedy.*

kindergarten for Cahaba residents. The Hewitt Elementary School on Chalkville Road housed grades one through nine.

As Trussville grew, R.G. Hewitt High School expanded to house students in grades seven through twelve, and Jefferson County contracted for a junior

Students participate in homecoming activities near Hewitt High School on Parkway Drive in the 1950s. *Trussville Historical Society.*

high school. At the same time, Hewitt Elementary School on Chalkville Road was overcrowded. The Hewitt Elementary School Annex on Cherokee Drive opened in 1969 for the second and third grades. The construction of that school was timely, as well as necessary, because the elementary school on Chalkville Road burned to the ground in May 1973. The fire happened during school hours at about 11:30 a.m., and all fourth, fifth and sixth grade students were evacuated. The students' bottle cap collection, a two-year process that was up to 937,000 bottle caps, was destroyed. The students were trying to collect 1 million bottle caps in a bin. Firemen from Trussville, Center Point, Birmingham and Springville worked to extinguish the fire, which would have likely spread to nearby homes had they not arrived in time. There were no injuries in the fire. For the remainder of that school year, classes took place in the Trussville Methodist Church and the nearby former First National Bank building. Portable classrooms were used for the 1973 fall term until additions could be made to the annex school on Cherokee Drive, which became the only elementary school in the city.

By the spring of 1979, the chances of a new high school building appeared likely, and the probable location was on forty acres of property between Interstate 59 and Green Drive. The Trussville City Council assured Jefferson

County officials that it would allocate twenty-five to thirty thousand gallons per day of wastewater treatment that a new school would require. With that assurance, Jefferson County commissioner Chriss Doss said the county was unofficially committed to putting up half the cost of extending a sewer line to the forty acres with the county school board footing the rest of the bill. The estimated total cost was $300,000.

The high school on Parkway Drive housed 700 students, but the proposed school on what is now Trussville-Clay Road would accommodate 1,500. In early August 1980, officials were still mulling over that location and another owned by Deerfoot Corp. on the Clay side of Interstate 59. By the end of that month, the Trussville-Clay Road location was determined to be the site for the new high school. The 130,000-square-foot building was designed by Adams, Benton and Peacher. Occupancy was planned for the fall of 1983. The building would contain thirty-two classrooms, a gymnasium with stage, a band room, a choral room, administrative offices, counseling offices, a library and a dining room. The school was to have a separate physical education area beside the gymnasium, with separate boys' and girls' dressing rooms, and a home economics laboratory with full sewing and food labs. An open courtyard was to be located outside the library and art room, complete with steps and a stage and a platform similar to an outdoor theater. Skylights and open courtyards would give the school a chance to get light into classrooms from inside, with few outside windows. The school planned for 1,200 students from Trussville and Clay to attend. Parking spaces for four hundred vehicles were included in the plans. The site's master plan's future construction projected room for a varsity football field, a field house, a baseball field, tennis courts, a stadium and stands.

In January 1981, the Jefferson County Board of Education voted to approve the purchase of the forty acres of property on Trussville-Clay Road for the new high school. Funds to build the high school came from the State Board of Education from the sale of $60 million in state bonds. Of that amount, Jefferson County received $3.1 million for the construction of the new high school.

In December 1983, the high school on Parkway Drive closed for the Christmas holiday. In January 1984, high school students began attending the new high school on Trussville-Clay Road. Later that year, in August, the Parkway Drive school building, built by the government in the 1930s, became the city's middle school for students in the fifth through seventh grades.

Construction of a multipurpose athletic complex next to the new Hewitt-Trussville High School began in May 1985. The six-thousand-square-foot

The New Deal–era school building on Parkway Drive first served as the high school and later the city's middle school. *Gary Lloyd.*

facility was built entirely with private funds, costing about $100,000. The new complex allowed the football team to have a dressing room and weight room on campus. The team was still driving to the Parkway Drive school for practice and workouts at the nearby stadium. At this time, construction was ongoing at the new high school for football and baseball practice fields.

In May 1985, the City of Birmingham proposed to annex 5,750 acres around Trussville and reaching along Interstate 59 almost to St. Clair County. The City of Trussville and Jefferson County Board of Education officials vowed to fight the proposed annexation because it would include the one-year-old high school. The school board's president, Kevin Walsh, said at the time that "we are at war with them." Three days after the city of Birmingham's proposal, about 1,500 area landowners asked the City of Trussville to annex their properties. On May 29, 1985, the City of Trussville annexed the school into its city limits.

In 1987, a classroom annex was constructed at Hewitt-Trussville Junior High School on Parkway Drive, a school that was originally built in 1964. The junior high school, which consisted of students in the eighth and ninth grades, was selected as one of the top secondary schools in the state of Alabama by state school superintendent Wayne Teague.

In October 1987, the Jefferson County Board of Education unanimously voted to change the name of Hewitt-Trussville Middle School to William E. Burkett Middle School, effective immediately. Burkett was the county's school superintendent from 1984 to 1989. Residents who opposed the name change presented their complaints the same week at the Trussville Community Center. Kevin Walsh had made the motion for the name change at a September 25, 1987 meeting. Within two weeks, he had told a crowd of Trussville residents that he would move to rescind his motion, a move that would change the name back to Hewitt-Trussville Middle School. One thousand people had signed petitions opposing the name being changed to William E. Burkett Middle School.

In 1990, Hewitt-Trussville High School was selected as one of the top 264 schools in the country by the U.S. Department of Education, the only public school in the state of Alabama to achieve the honor. The award was based on all-around excellence. For that year, Hewitt-Trussville had a superior band and choral groups, a great Science Olympiad and Scholar's Bowl teams and an outstanding sports program.

In late 1991, a feasibility study was started by the state board of education to find out if the City of Trussville could financially support a school system independent of county tax money. At the time, there were 4,800 total students enrolled at Hewitt Elementary, Hewitt-Trussville Middle, Hewitt-Trussville Junior High and Hewitt-Trussville High Schools. A move toward its own school system at the time would force nearly half the enrollment—835 students at Clay Elementary School and 1,247 at Chalkville Elementary School—to find an alternative to Hewitt-Trussville Middle School when reaching the seventh grade. Those two elementary schools at the time were feeder schools to the middle school. Reducing the number of students in Trussville would help with overcrowding from the growing city.

In early 1992, a group of parents from the Clay and Chalkville areas formed Save Our Schools, a group in opposition of the city's forming its own school system. According to Jefferson County Board of Education figures, 62 percent of the students attending the four Trussville schools lived outside the city. A report from the Alabama Department of Education in March 1992 said Trussville could financially support its own school system, with an annual operating budget of about $13 million if appropriate taxes were raised. That budget amount assumed Trussville residents approving a fifteen-millage property tax increase that would generate about $450,000 annually. Under that plan, nonresident students could stay in Trussville schools.

In April 1992, the Trussville City Council tapped a five-member school panel to serve as the city's first school board, its first task negotiating with the Jefferson County School System for a solution to overcrowding. Another chief responsibility of the new school panel was to seek clearance from the U.S. Justice Department to operate a school system should the board decide to move toward taking control of the four Trussville schools. The five appointed to the school board were former Trussville city councilman Dennis Hill, Donna Cornelius, Terry Fleck, Don Haisten and Cecil Medders. All were members of the city's eleven-member education committee.

On September 29, 1992, an eight-millage property tax hike was approved, a measure that could generate $9.6 million each year. Hill recommended to the Trussville City Council that it abolish the newly formed school board, but Mayor Charles Grover and Councilman Gerald Glenn said they did not support abolishing the board immediately. Charles Grover said that he would recommend that the board be inactive while a lawsuit over the eight-millage property tax increase was resolved. After about a year of planning and discussion, Trussville did not form its own school system and remained as part of the Jefferson County School System.

The millage increase that had been approved, however, remained and helped ease the overcrowding of Trussville schools. Jefferson County school superintendent Bruce Wright announced in April 1993 that the county would build a high school instead of an elementary school in the Hewitt-Clay-Chalkville zone. The three-phase, ten-year repair and construction project was made possible by the eight-millage property tax increase that had been approved. Wright's plan included building a high school and middle school in the Clay-Chalkville area to serve students who would have otherwise been routed to schools in Trussville. The schools would be completed in about two years. The plan would reduce enrollment at Hewitt-Trussville High School from 1,234 students to about 1,029 students. The new middle school in Clay would be fed from Chalkville Elementary School and Clay Elementary School. The new middle school would reduce the number of students attending Hewitt-Trussville Middle School from 1,107 students to 834 students.

As a result of two new schools being constructed, the plan in Trussville called for Hewitt Elementary School, which served grades one through four, to become Hewitt Primary School and serve kindergarten through the second grade. The plan also called for Hewitt-Trussville Middle School, which was serving grades five through seven, to become Hewitt Elementary School and serve grades three through five. Hewitt-Trussville Junior High School would change to the middle school and serve grades six through eight, and the high school would hold students in the ninth through twelfth grades. There would no longer be a junior high school in Trussville under this plan.

The possibility of change had little apparent effect on Hewitt-Trussville High School's students in 1993. The school that year won the U.S.

Department of Education's Blue Ribbon School award, one of only two others in the state of Alabama to do so. The school wouldn't be able to apply again for the award for four years, about when a new high school in the Clay-Chalkville area would be up and running. "I think it will be a challenge, after the division is made, to go for it again," Principal Connie Williams said at the time.

The Jefferson County Board of Education pursued six options for the two new schools in Clay, but difficulty finding the best site pushed back construction and opening. The plan was to have a site selected by the end of 1993 and construction of the new schools completed by the end of the 1995–96 school year. In the fall of 1993, Hewitt-Trussville Middle School was already using two outdoor portable classrooms to combat overcrowding. The middle school in 1993 housed 1,176 students. Classes were composed of thirty students on average, an increase of four students per classroom from the previous school year.

Clay-Chalkville High School and Clay-Chalkville Middle School opened for the 1996–97 school year. In 1995, the Jefferson County Board of Education had given the community a $750,000 line of credit toward developing athletic fields. The unincorporated Clay-Chalkville community had no official city to look to for money. The old Shades Valley High School steel-frame football stadium was transplanted and reerected behind Clay-Chalkville High School and is now known as Cougar Stadium. The transplant gave Clay-Chalkville High School a stadium that seated five to six thousand people for less money than it would have cost to build a new concrete stadium. It cost between $225,000 and $250,000 to move the stadium, roughly $200,000 less than building new concrete bleachers. Some of the $750,000 line of credit went toward other fields, such as one for baseball.

In early 1996, it was predicted that Hewitt-Trussville High School would lose about 200 of its 1,480 students to the new Clay-Chalkville High School. It was projected that over the next few years, a total of about 400 students would move from Hewitt-Trussville High School to Clay-Chalkville High School. That breathing room, it was predicted, would allow Hewitt-Trussville High School to again accommodate ninth-grade students. Despite the breathing room, Trussville maintained its elementary, middle, junior high and high schools. In late 1998 and early 1999, that dynamic began to change. A sinkhole along the edge of Parkway Drive near Hewitt-Trussville Junior High School created an emergency for the city. A sinkhole is a depression in the ground caused by the dissolving of underground rock formations. The

City of Trussville has dealt with many sinkholes in the Cahaba Project area, notably on popular streets and on one of the tennis courts on the Mall. A stone culvert installed in the 1930s with the Cahaba Project near the sinkhole was believed to be the cause of the sinkhole. The culvert could have been leaking water and making the sinkhole larger.

The Trussville City Council in the spring of 1999 approved $234,995 for Veterans Landscaping to open a wide hole in the ground and plug the hole near its bottom, which would create a rock bridge to support dirt and other materials dumped to fill the hole. Once the digging started, the landscaping company discovered offshoots of the original sinkhole that extended under the junior high school property, near the Cahaba River. The junior high school's cafeteria and library were demolished as a result of the sinkhole. Two portable classrooms became the school's makeshift cafeteria and library. Students ate in their classrooms and only a limited number of students were allowed in the portable library at one time. In August 1999, the Jefferson County School System agreed to spend $70,000 to fix a new sinkhole found that month. That sinkhole was found behind the restrooms of the annex. Bhate Engineering filled the sinkhole with grout and drove eight timber pilings down to the bedrock to stabilize the annex's foundation. Ninth graders were moved up to the high school and eighth graders were moved down to the middle school on Parkway Drive. By the fall of 2002, the junior high school, which had been constructed thirty-eight years prior, was no longer in use. By 2005, all that was left of the junior high was the rear annex and gymnasium, now used for Trussville Parks and Recreation games and events. A section of the rear annex also houses what is now the Trussville City Schools Alternative Learning Center.

Another significant change was announced in July 1999, when Amerex Corporation founders Ned and Goldie Paine planned to donate property along U.S. Highway 11 near their company on the condition it be used for a new elementary school. The Jefferson County Board of Education, which had approved a new elementary school to ease overcrowding at Hewitt Elementary School, accepted the thirty-eight-acre donation. The school board had previously run into trouble finding available land in Trussville for the new school. The school board planned to spend between $8 and $9 million for the new school, not including the $2 million value of the property. The first plan was for the school to accommodate nine hundred students and open in 2001. In the fall of 2000, Hewitt Elementary School consisted of eleven kindergarten classes, thirteen first-grade classes, twelve second-grade classes, thirteen fourth-grade classes and three special education classes. At

Paine Primary School serves Trussville's youngest students. *Gary Lloyd.*

the time, only four of the school's forty-eight kindergarten to third-grade classes met the state standard of one teacher for every eighteen pupils in elementary classes. There were six portable trailers and one modular building at the lower part of the school's campus. The school's lunch period in 2000 began at 10:00 a.m. and lasted just over three hours to accommodate all the classes. All of this led in part to the need for a new school and Ned and Goldie Paine's donation.

The City of Trussville and Jefferson County School System differed early on in regard to which grades the second new school on U.S. Highway 11 would house. The county was already set to pay for the kindergarten through second-grade school, now Paine Primary School, through state funds. The county wanted an intermediate school to consist of students in the third through fifth grades, while Trussville wanted it to hold grades four through six. Trussville mayor Gene Melton said at the time that the city was willing to spend up to $10 million to build a three-grade elementary school. He also asked the Jefferson County Board of Education to use bond money to pay for another elementary school. The school board was set to build the K–2 school with funds carrying a debt Trussville would have kept had it split from the county to form its own school system.

In March 2001, the Jefferson County Board of Education approved a $19.7 million school construction contract for Gary C. Wyatt Inc. of Birmingham to build two new elementary schools in Trussville. The agreement stated that the City of Trussville and the county school board would jointly pay for a kindergarten through second-grade school and a grades three to five school to be built on a forty-one-acre parcel along U.S. Highway 11. The county's share of the payment was $10 million for the primary school, while Trussville's was $9.7 million for what is now known as Paine Intermediate School. At the time, it was predicted that about 1,600 students would fill the 105 classrooms between the two schools, which were set to open for the start of the 2002–03 school year.

In April 2001, however, the county school board approved an $18 million deal in which the City of Trussville would pay $10 million for the intermediate school and the county would finance the primary school for $8 million. The deal replaced Hewitt Elementary School with two smaller schools. The old elementary school became and still is the administration office for the Trussville Fire Department. The offices are located in the old kindergarten building, and the main building became the Lewis "Cooter" Simpson Training Facility, named for the man who has been a member of the fire department since 1957, was member of the police department from 1959 to 1969 and headed the city's streets and sanitations department from 1988 to his retirement in 2013.

Ned Paine broke the first bit of ground in August 2001 for the new schools. The schools were set to open officially in January 2003, with about 860 students at Paine Primary School and 850 students at Paine Intermediate School. With the opening of the Paine schools, Hewitt Elementary School and Hewitt-Trussville Junior High School were officially closed.

Paine Intermediate School is located beside Paine Primary School. *Gary Lloyd.*

The subtraction of the junior high school meant an addition for Hewitt-Trussville Middle School on Parkway Drive. A $1.1 million addition that included eight classrooms was constructed so that eighth-grade students could attend the middle school. The addition allowed the school to cease the use of ten portable classrooms.

In early 2002, the City of Trussville proposed an increase in its sales tax to allow the city to create a reserve fund for a school system. The hike discussed was a one-cent increase, bringing the city's sales tax to eight cents on every dollar spent. The Trussville City Council approved the increase in January 2002 and speculated that it could mean an additional $3.5 million per year. The city planned to use about $900,000 of that per year to pay its incurred debt to build one of the Paine schools.

In May 2002, a consultant recommended that Trussville form its own school system by 2004, citing a financial feasibility report that showed the city could form a school system with an initial $17.8 million operating budget and 2,800 students in its first year without raising property taxes. The city over the past two years had been seriously considering forming its own school system. Gene Melton had said, however, he would like Trussville to have at least $20 million in reserve funds before breaking away from the Jefferson County School System.

In July 2002, the Trussville City Council voted to spend $132,600 toward the construction of right and left turn lanes on U.S. Highway 11 at the Paine schools campus. In November of the same year, an unexpected cost emerged when it was determined that a slope at the site of the new schools needed repair, a cost of $552,010 that the City of Trussville and the Jefferson County Board of Education split. The slope erosion problem had worsened by January 2003, delaying the move of students from Hewitt Elementary School to the Paine campus. The Paine schools officially opened their doors for teachers and students at the beginning of the 2003–04 school year.

Trussville Breaks from Jefferson County

According to an updated feasibility study in early 2004, it was predicted that Trussville could start an $18 million school system with nearly three thousand students as early as the fall of 2005. The Alabama Senate in April 2004 voted twenty-one to zero to authorize a bill that allowed Trussville to hold a property tax referendum and annex certain property. The proposal centered on equalizing property taxes paid by Trussville residents in Jefferson and St. Clair Counties. The vote failed in November 2004 and would have meant a millage increase for Trussville homeowners.

In May 2004, the Trussville City Council established and appointed a five-member school board. It again included Dennis Hill. The other four members were Butch Howard, former mayor Ormond Bentley, Ned Paine and John Floyd. The school board's first task was to select a superintendent, and it hired consultant Bob Mitchell, the first superintendent of Hoover City Schools, to aid in the process. In August 2004, the newly formed Trussville City Board of Education revealed three finalists for the superintendent position. They were Cullman City Schools superintendent Suzanne Freeman, Tallapoosa County Schools assistant superintendent Charles Ledbetter and Russell County Schools director of instruction Janet Womack. Sixteen applications had been received for the job.

Suzanne Freeman earned a doctorate in curriculum and teaching from Auburn University and had worked for Auburn City Schools as an assistant superintendent and principal for the Auburn Early Education Center. She had been the Cullman City Schools superintendent since 2000. At the time, Ledbetter was completing his doctorate at Auburn University. He had worked as an administrative assistant, teacher and coach in the Tallapoosa County and Walker County School Systems. Womack had previously been an elementary school principal at Russell County Schools, after earning a doctorate in curriculum and teaching from Auburn University.

The Trussville City Board of Education later in August selected Suzanne Freeman as the first superintendent of Trussville City Schools. She was chosen over the other finalists largely because of her experience in already leading a school system. Freeman's contract was approved in October 2004, paying her $125,000 per year over a four-year period. The contract included a one-year automatic renewal clause that the school board could exercise if it was happy with Freeman's work.

Just two months into Freeman's job, the Trussville City Board of Education's long-term capital improvements plan showed the school system could build a new high school and turn the high school on Trussville-Clay Road into a middle school. The plan called for building the new high school by 2008, turn the high school on Trussville-Clay Road into a school for grades six through eight and convert the historic school on Parkway Drive into an elementary school by 2010. The plan indicated that enrollment in Trussville schools could have around 8,200 students by 2034. The plan, Suzanne Freeman said at the time, was to use the $37 million it expected to receive from Jefferson County's one-cent sales tax increase to build a new high school and complete other projects. In December 2004, just a month after the property tax referendum failed, the school board agreed to pay $65,838 to nine companies for the renovation of the former Hewitt Kindergarten Annex on North Chalkville Road, in the same area where the elementary school burned in 1973. The building became and remains the Trussville City Schools Central Office.

The school board in February 2005 approved the long-term capital improvements plan, which showed that Trussville could have four elementary schools, a new high school and a larger middle school in the future. In March 2005, the Trussville and Jefferson County Boards of Education agreed to key details for Trussville's school system formation, including the transfer of four county schools and about four thousand students to the new system. A federal judge, U.S. district court judge Inge Johnson, ruled in May 2005 that Trussville could establish its own school system without adversely affecting court-supervised desegregation agreements in nearby systems.

The Trussville City Board of Education in July 2005 chose Davis Architects to design a new high school with an estimated cost of $40 million. At the time, the school board was considering two locations off Trussville-Clay Road for the new high school, which would be constructed to house 1,600 students with the possibility to expand and house 2,400 students.

School officials later in 2005 found out that the cost of building the new high school was an estimated $55 million. That cost included construction of a 285,000-square-foot campus, a contingency fund, landscaping, money for architect fees, money for construction manager fees and funds for school furnishings. The high school, built in a heavily wooded area between Trussville-Clay Road and Deerfoot Parkway, was completed in 2008. Students moved to the school after fall break in October. The general contractor for the new school was Doster Construction Company, which built the 361,000-square-foot, $70 million facility, which sits on roughly seventy-eight acres near the Cahaba River. The building's exterior was constructed to feature a mixture of colored brick, ground-face block and fieldstone with large, expansive windows. The interior was designed to incorporate extensive daylight through the windows to show off the polished concrete floors with accents of carpet in offices and ceramic tile in the restrooms. The high school contains about seventy classrooms, two gymnasiums, band and choral halls and the Performing Arts Center, a 1,180-seat theater used for pageants, plays and other functions. Development of the site also included all utilities, access roads, storm water collection with a retention structure and parking for eight hundred vehicles. Built to be a "green" school, Hewitt-Trussville High School is thought to be one of the most environmentally friendly schools in the state of Alabama.

By July 2012, the Trussville City Board of Education unanimously approved a contract settlement with Suzanne Freeman, ending her seven years as the first superintendent of Trussville City Schools. The most well-known reason for Freeman's dismissal was the resignation of Hewitt-Trussville High School principal Zack Barnes in early July 2012. Barnes had only been at the high school for one year. He left to take the same position at Homewood High School. Barnes was the fifth principal of Hewitt-Trussville High School in the school system's seven-year history, and many citizens and parents of students were not happy with the turnover. Suzanne Freeman's settlement contract nullified her four-year contract and committed the school board to pay her $600,000 over a two-year period. If Freeman was to be hired as the superintendent of another school system before June 30, 2014, her compensation would be reduced by the amount of pay she would receive from a new job. The agreement also called for her to serve as an administrative officer for Trussville through 2014, a position that allowed Freeman to continue in the state's teacher retirement system and keep her health insurance. Suzanne Freeman had been earning $202,000 per year as part of her contract.

The Trussville City Board of Education wasted little time in naming Freeman's replacement. Just over a week after Freeman's contract settlement was approved, the school board, made up of Bill Roberts, Danny Garrett, Sid McNeal, Stan Garrett and Gayle Glenn, tapped Pattie Neill as its interim superintendent. Her interim contract began on July 30, 2012, and would pay her $78,000 over a six-month period. In November 2012, the school board approved Neill as the school system's permanent superintendent, with a contract set to end in June 2016. The board of education agreed to provide notice in December 2015 if the contract would not be renewed. If it were renewed, it would automatically be extended for one year. Neill was the superintendent of the Cumberland County School District in Crossville, Tennessee, from 2003 to 2007. From then to her appointment as Trussville City Schools' superintendent, she served as an assistant professor of graduate studies at Samford University in Birmingham, where she oversaw elementary and secondary teachers earning master's and doctorate degrees in education. In August 2013, the Trussville City Board of Education released its first evaluation of Neill as a superintendent, rating her job performance as a 4.70 on a 5.00-point scale. The evaluation covered forty-two areas of criteria across ten categories, which were scored individually and independently by the five school board members. Neill received a composite score of 4.00 or above in every category, including thirteen in which she received a perfect score. In Freeman's last evaluation as superintendent, released in August 2011, she earned an overall 4.01 out of 5.00.

The year 2013 was a busy and productive one for the Trussville City Schools system. The board of education that May approved plans for two new elementary schools—one near the Magnolia Place subdivision and the other in the original high school and former middle school on Parkway Drive. The historic school had been vacated by middle school students in 2008 when the new high school opened, allowing middle school students to move into the former high school on Trussville-Clay Road. The new schools were approved due to overcrowding at Paine Primary School and Paine Intermediate School. Paine Primary School's capacity is 774 students, but it housed 913 kids during the 2012–13 school year. It used five outdoor portable classrooms for that school year. Paine Intermediate School has a capacity of 785 students but housed 941 kids and used eight portable classrooms during the 2012–13 school year. Each of the new schools, planned to open in 2015, will house roughly 400 students with the ability to accommodate about 500 each. Both schools were to be constructed with Federal Emergency Management Agency–approved community tornado shelters in case of a natural disaster. Building a new school near Magnolia Place and renovating the historic school on Parkway Drive came with a price tag of between $18 and $19 million. Funding the schools was likely to be contingent on the approval of a seven-millage property tax increase in the city of Trussville.

Chapter 7

CHURCHES

Churches, both big and small, are located all over the city of Trussville. The importance of the church in Trussville is obvious, as evidenced by how quickly one was established in 1821, not long after the Trussville area was settled. Cahawba Baptist Church was constituted by Elder Sion Blythe, an itinerant preacher of the county, and nine other men and women on July 14, 1821, one month previous to Warren Truss's first purchase of land in the Trussville region. One of the earliest formed churches in Jefferson County, Cahawba Baptist Church was identified with the Mount Zion Association, which was organized in 1823. The church withdrew from the association in 1833, becoming one of nine constituent churches that formed the Canaan Association. In early 1827, Cahawba Baptist Church was a one-room building forty feet long and twenty-six feet wide with nine feet between joists. The first building was located south of U.S. Highway 11 near the railroad tracks, land that belonged to J. Warren Truss, who on October 6, 1827, gave a parcel of land to the church so that it could continue. The church was strict with its members, who were dismissed for minuscule infractions and only readmitted with the approval of the church. Warren Truss in 1826 had been excluded from the church for being intoxicated with spirituous liquors. Slaves were taken into membership until after the Civil War began. In 1867, the slaves were dismissed from Cahawba Baptist Church to form a church of their own, with the provision that they were not to be received again into membership of Cahawba Baptist Church.

When the Alabama and Chattanooga Railroad came to the Trussville area in 1870, the church helped the railroad company find a site for a depot so as to not interfere with the nearby church. Two years later, however, a new building was constructed to serve as the new church, and its first service was held in October 1873.

In April 1888, the name, which had become Cahaba Baptist Church, was changed to Trussville Baptist Church. All Sunday school classes met in the sanctuary until 1911, when three rooms were built across the back of the church. The church suffered heavy damage in 1921 as a result of a tornado. It blew off a portion of the roof, including the steeple and bell tower. Repairs were made and services continued as usual, with a new façade that included four white columns. The Great Depression was hard on Cahaba Baptist Church and all churches, and in 1937, the church began using a planned budget, an appropriate time because it also hired its first full-time pastor, Preston Acker, the same year.

The Baptist church reaped the benefits of the Cahaba Project's construction in the late 1930s, as it experienced a growth in population. The church's first vacation Bible school began in 1938 and construction of a new, bigger church building commenced in 1946. For a brief period, the congregation met at Hewitt Elementary School. In March 1954, the church's name was changed to the First Baptist Church of Trussville, which it remains today.

A look at First Baptist Church of Trussville, one of the largest churches in the area. *Gary Lloyd.*

The year 1962 was significant for First Baptist Church of Trussville. It opened a kindergarten, transferred the Baptist cemetery to the Trussville Memorial Cemetery Association and placed a historical marker on the site of the church that opened in 1873. In 1983, the church sold its pastorium on Main Street, and youth activities—Bible Blasts, summer trips and mission activities—increased in popularity throughout the 1980s.

First Baptist Church of Trussville on North Chalkville Road today is one of the largest churches in the city. Its ministries include a weekday preschool ministry, as well as ministries for children, middle school–aged youths, adult small groups, senior adults, high school youths, recreation/events, counseling, singles, missions, library, media and conservatory. The staff includes more than forty employees. Worship services are at 9:15 a.m. and 10:45 a.m. on Sundays and 6:00 p.m. on Wednesdays.

Trussville First Presbyterian Church

The First Presbyterian Church of Trussville, located on U.S. Highway 11, dates back to October 2, 1867, when several people met at Sarah Talley's residence with the Reverend D.Y. Wyatt, the Reverend A.M. Sadler and the Reverend T.B. Taylor for the purpose of organizing the Cave Springs

Trussville First Presbyterian Church on U.S. Highway 11. *Ron Burkett.*

congregation of the Cumberland Presbyterian Church. At the next meeting of the Presbytery of Springville, Alabama, the church's name, Synod, was changed to Montneba, or Mt. Nebo. The land on which the church was erected was given to the Presbyterians by Latham Linder for $1 in 1868, with the stipulation that it would be used for church purposes or revert back to the donor or his heirs. Adjoining land was given to a Masonic organization and a frame house costing $175 was built to be jointly occupied by the Masons and the church congregation. The frame house served the congregation until 1899, when it was demolished and the present-day structure was built nearby.

On October 25, 1958, the congregation changed the church's name from Mt. Nebo Presbyterian Church to First Presbyterian Church of Trussville, which it remains today. The church is highly visible from U.S. Highway 11, a white wooden building with light blue outlining the windows.

First United Methodist Church of Trussville

The Trussville Methodist Episcopal Church, formed through the efforts of Nancy Jane Truss Reed and Francis Mitchell Grace, came into being during the Reconstruction era in 1869, though it was first formed as a Methodist society in 1848. Grace was the first listed minister of the church. Other charter members of this church were Enos Truss Vann, Elizabeth Faust Vann and Williams Jackson Reed. The framed church was built in the late 1800s and painted white. It was built on the former Hewitt Elementary School playground, the trees serving then as hitching posts and wagon scotches. The church had a tall steeple with a big bell that was tolled when there was a death, funeral, Sunday school, church service and other gatherings of people. The building's one room was partitioned for Sunday school rooms with curtains hung on wires, and the building's interior was lit by oil lamps on the walls between the windows. A circle of lamps hung from the ceiling.

Services were held at the Methodist church until 1938, when the land and school building nearby were exchanged for the church property. Around $1,000 was spent to turn the school into a church. Services began at the new church in May 1938. The Trussville Methodist Church had the first organized choir in Trussville, and it performed at Trussville Baptist Church and Mt. Nebo Presbyterian Church. In 1954, Trussville Methodist Church added an educational building for a cost of around $80,000. By 1960, the converted

First United Methodist Church of Trussville sits in the heart of Trussville on North Chalkville Road. *Gary Lloyd.*

The Trussville Church of Christ, on Talley Street, began meeting in 1941. *Gary Lloyd.*

schoolhouse was torn down and ground was broken for a new sanctuary, which was completed by Easter Sunday in 1960 at a cost of $160,000. The church was remodeled in 1969 at a cost of more than $90,000. That same year, the church membership was at 742 people, and 405 were enrolled in the church's school.

First United Methodist Church of Trussville's Family Life Center opened in 1985, a youth building was constructed in 2004 and a new playground was installed behind the church building in 2007. The Family Life Center received a facelift in 2011.

Holy Infant of Prague Catholic Church

Holy Infant of Prague Catholic Church began in 1939 when John A. Bratton celebrated Mass twice per month in a vacant apartment in the Cahaba Project. The 1940 census showed that 50 Catholic families resided in the Trussville area. In 1941, Bishop Toolen appointed Frank Giri as the first pastor in preparation for the building of the church. Land was purchased on Hewitt Street beside present-day First Baptist Church of Trussville, and ground was broken on August 31, 1941. The church was dedicated on May 10, 1942, by Bishop Toolen. The church's first resident pastor was the Reverend Joseph Adams, who was appointed on June 21, 1947. James Gallagher, who became pastor in 1951, built the Parish Hall. Holy Infant of Prague Catholic Church consisted of around 100 to 125 families from 1969 until 1987.

The construction of a new church was completed in 2006. The church relocated from the Hewitt Street location, now a parking lot area belonging to First Baptist Church of Trussville, to a Gadsden Highway location on September 23, 2006. The new building includes a parish hall and classrooms. The present-day membership totals more than nine hundred families and continues to grow. Holy Infant of Prague Catholic Church is also the annual site of Oktoberfest, a German festival that includes food, live music and other activities.

Trussville Church of Christ

The Trussville Church of Christ began meeting on July 3, 1941, with the help of John T. Lewis, D.N. Wallace, the West End Church of Christ and the Woodlawn Church of Christ. Not long after the church formed, funds were raised and property was purchased to build the church in Trussville. The church building on Talley Street, just off North Chalkville Road, was completed in 1947, between the First United Methodist and First Baptist Churches. Major modifications of the building were completed in the 1960s, and additional remodeling was done in the 1980s. The present building, still on Talley Street, was completed in 2005 and is a modification of the original. Early members of the Trussville Church of Christ included the Wade, Waid, Watson, Underwood, Postlethwaite, Whitehead, Harris and Hackworth families. The Trussville Church of Christ was also instrumental in the beginnings of similar churches in Clay and Pinson.

Southside Baptist Church

Southside Baptist Church on Roper Road on the south end of the city of Trussville got its start on August 24, 1941, when the church was organized as the Tabernacle Missionary Baptist Church. The church's original members included fourteen people, and the first organizational meeting was held on August 27, 1941. The church was accepted into the St. Clair Association in October 1941. Arthur Tillman, from the Happy Hollow community, was elected as pastor in August 1942. A longtime resident of the Trussville area, Arthur Tillman was known for performing marriage ceremonies in Trussville, Argo and Springville. He remained the pastor for three years. The first vacation Bible school at Tabernacle Missionary Baptist Church was held in the summer of 1946.

The original church building was large enough to hold three hundred people, despite its not being furnished with enough seating for that many. It was decided that a smaller building should be constructed, and churchgoers began to meet in it in 1949. The name of the church was changed to Trussville Southside Baptist Church in 1952, and by the spring of 1960, the new building was completely finished. Southside Baptist Church is still located on Roper Road, just across from Queenstown Road.

The Episcopal Church of the Holy Cross

A small group of Episcopalians began to meet in Trussville early in 1942. The group petitioned the Bishop of Alabama to allow it to form a church, and the bishop accepted. The first service was held at Mt. Nebo Presbyterian

Church, and other services were held in homes, the community center and the high school. The church's first building was built in 1955, and a new worship space and office wing were added late in 1984. The Episcopal Church of the Holy Cross is still located in Trussville on Parkway Drive not far from the Cahaba River.

Other Baptist Churches

There are about eight other Baptist churches that serve the Trussville area. Midway Baptist Church sits at the top of Chalkville Mountain Road near a large commercial district. It was founded on October 5, 1952, with the Reverend J.L. Beaty serving as pastor. The building was dedicated on October 3, 1965, when the Reverend John E. Harper was pastor. In 2013, Purpose Life Church began meeting at Midway Baptist Church.

Mt. Joy Baptist Church is located on Valley Road, directly across from the Forties area. The historical church was founded in 1857 and provides a contemporary worship flare and vision for future growth. The church offers pastoral counseling, Bible study, couples' ministry, music ministry, youth ministry, praise/dance ministry, bell choir ministry, usher/greeters ministry and Sunday school.

Ridgecrest Baptist Church constituted on September 9, 1956, and met in Center Point until October 14, 2007. The church's members met in a transitional facility until they relocated to the church's current location on Gadsden Highway in Trussville on August 17, 2008.

NorthPark Baptist Church, located on Deerfoot Parkway, dates back to 1955, when it was Roebuck Park Baptist Church. After a brief period of decline, the congregation decided to relocate to Trussville, meeting at Hewitt-Trussville High School for two years. The name of the church was changed to NorthPark Baptist Church and forty acres of land were purchased on Deerfoot Parkway. On November 3, 2002, the church held its first worship service at the new facility. The church broke ground in 2005 on a forty-three-thousand-square-foot education addition that houses the church's preschool, children's ministry and youth ministry. The church also added a three-hundred-seat balcony to its worship center, a coffee shop in the lobby and two hundred more parking spaces. As of 2013, the church's membership totaled 4,261 people.

CrossPoint Church on Liles Lane in Trussville was first introduced to the First Baptist Church of Center Point as an idea on October 25, 1998.

The idea was to create a new satellite campus. On February 26, 2000, land was purchased, and within eighteen months, the church paid for the twenty-five acres and plans were developed for the church structure. On July 8, 2002, more than two hundred volunteers from eleven states began Phase 1 of construction. CrossPoint Church began its ministry on April 6, 2003. By August 2004, it was suggested that CrossPoint and First Baptist Church of Center Point were heading in different directions, and CrossPoint transformed from a satellite campus to a mission church. The church became independent on January 2, 2005, and identified as a Southern Baptist church. There were about 290 families that were accepted as new members. By November 2005, it was announced that more than 100 families had joined since February 2005, and another building was completed in February 2007. CrossPoint then opened a recreation facility in late 2007, which holds two full basketball courts and a walking track.

Highland View Missionary Baptist Church is located off Roper Road on the south end of Trussville. It was organized on November 6, 1949, and the Reverend Billy L. Walker was the founder, builder and pastor. The church is still located here today.

Sulphur Springs Baptist Church is also located on Roper Road in Trussville, not far from the St. Clair County line. The church building was dedicated in December 2003, but the adjoining Sulphur Springs Cemetery was established in 1866. This church holds worship services on Sunday mornings, Sunday evenings and Wednesday evenings.

Deerfoot Baptist Church is located on Mount Olive Church Road, not far from Hewitt-Trussville High School. Dr. Roger Willmore has been the pastor since February 2005. The church serves preschool-aged children, students, young adults and adults. The church also has a library and child development center.

Another Methodist Church

Clearbranch United Methodist Church was chartered in 1996, initially meeting in a home with an average attendance of 45 people. In less than a year, meetings were taking place at a local school, and by the end of 1997, attendance was up to 250 people. In 1998, ground was broken on Glenn Road near Interstate 59 for a twenty-thousand-square-foot multipurpose building, and in 1999, the church added a second Sunday morning service to accommodate the growing number of people who were attending. A new building was dedicated in 2002, and by 2004, the average attendance had climbed to more than 1,500 people. Clearbranch United Methodist Church remains a popular church in the area today.

Other Presbyterian Churches

Eastminster Presbyterian Church, located on U.S. Highway 11 in Trussville, was founded as Seventy-sixth Street Presbyterian Church in 1891. The church has ministered to the city of Trussville at the U.S. Highway 11 location since 1992. In May 2013, however, Eastminster Presbyterian Church's congregation began worshipping at the newer Grace Presbyterian Church location on Deerfoot Parkway in Trussville. Grace has a large worship facility, while services at Eastminster Presbyterian Church were held in a gymnasium. At a May 5, 2013 worship and communion service at Eastminster, a bell outside the church was rung twenty-two times to honor the twenty-two years the church provided services in Trussville.

The merger of Eastminster and Grace came about after many town hall meetings over the course of a couple of years. The merged churches became Cahaba Springs Presbyterian Church, and on August 4, 2013, the Reverend Shelaine Bird, the previous transitional pastor at Chapel in the Pines Presbyterian Church in Hoover, became the new church's pastor. With the merger came the closing of Eastminster Presbyterian Church's preschool program, though Cahaba Springs enrolled some of those students, from infants to pre-kindergarteners. The Eastminster building was under an option contract with a commercial real estate developer in late 2013. Cahaba Springs planned to lease or buy a multipurpose facility in Trussville to continue programs such as Zumba classes and concerts.

Other Churches

The Trussville Church of God was built on Vann Circle in 1955 and was later remodeled and renovated. The Trussville Church of the Nazarene was located on Vann Circle until the early 1940s. New Life Church and New Harbor Souls Conquering Church are located within a few hundred yards of each other on Service Road in Trussville. Vann Valley Assembly of God, located on Trussville-Clay Road, changed its name in 2012 to Restoration Church. It is still in the same location today, not far from the Trussville Civic Center. St. Joseph Anglican Church on Cavern Road was founded in January 2009. The church prides itself on forming relationships and worships in conformance with Holy Scripture using the 1928 Book of Common Prayer.

In 2004, Matt Pitt, a 2001 Hewitt-Trussville High School graduate, founded the Basement, a ministry for youth. It was called so because after dealing with a drug overdose in college, Pitt began a ministry in the basement of his parents' home in Roebuck. The Basement outgrew churches in Springville, Trussville and Center Point, drawing thousands at times to the Church of the Highlands in Irondale and the Boutwell Auditorium in downtown Birmingham. The Basement was considered to be one of the top rising ministries in the country. In May 2012, however, Pitt's sport utility vehicle was pulled over in Calera, Alabama, for allegedly flashing blue lights at other cars, causing them to pull over. When Pitt was pulled over by authorities, he allegedly showed police a badge he had received and, according to police, identified himself as a Jefferson County sheriff's deputy. Pitt was charged with impersonating a peace officer, and in September 2012, he pleaded guilty to attempting to impersonate an officer, a plea that carried a suspended sentence of one year in jail with two years of unsupervised probation. He paid a $1,000 fine and apologized to Calera police.

It was announced in August 2013 by the Jefferson County Sheriff's Office that Pitt had been charged again with impersonating an officer, stemming from a June 15, 2013 incident in which Pitt allegedly picked up a rifle near a wooded area in Grayson Valley while riding an all-terrain vehicle, identifying himself to a man as a law enforcement officer. Pitt was charged again and his probation from the first charge was revoked in October 2013 by a Shelby County Circuit Court judge, meaning he'd have to spend the next ten months in the Shelby County jail. While in jail, Pitt had phone privileges, using the opportunity each week to call in to the Basement services, which are held at an office building off Main Street in Trussville. A cellphone would be connected to a sound system, and when Pitt called in, his voice would be heard over the sound system, often reading announcements, encouraging followers and talking about life in jail. Most of Pitt's phone calls lasted fifteen or fewer minutes. In a YouTube video posted in October 2013, Pitt said that he believed that God was using the Basement and himself to reach Shelby County jail inmates and that God sent him inside the jail walls to minister to them. On December 9, 2013, a Jefferson County District Court judge sent Pitt's case to a grand jury for review.

Miracle Hill Church is a small church located on Smith Sims Road on the city's south end, where Scott Cherry is pastor. The Healing Place Church originated in May 1967 in the Roebuck area. The church, which began relocating to Trussville in 2005, rented the former Hewitt-Trussville High School—now Hewitt-Trussville Middle School—on Trussville-Clay Road to hold its services until it sold its building. Due to renovations at the school's auditorium, the church rented a building off Happy Hollow Road to hold its Sunday and Wednesday services until the construction of its new, permanent building was completed. The church moved into its new church building on Trussville-Clay Road in December 2007. Since that time, the Healing Place Church has undergone two additional phases—expanding the parking lot and adding a new children's and youth wing, which was completed in September 2013. Another construction phase, for a new sanctuary, is planned for the future of the church, which consists of 1,800 members.

Faith Community Fellowship Church is located on Gadsden Highway, not far from the Paine Elementary Campus. The church features multiple ministries and life groups, which are small groups of people who share something in common along with a desire to learn about and grow in their relationships with Jesus Christ.

Deerfoot Community Bible Church is located on Deerfoot Parkway, close to Cahaba Springs Presbyterian Church. George Maronge Jr. has been the church's pastor for twenty years.

Chapter 8

INDUSTRY AND BUSINESS

Like most southern cities, Trussville got its start as a rural, isolated community, the major occupation being farming, though the 1870 census numbers show two physicians, two store clerks, one miller and three schoolteachers. That same year, the railroad reached Trussville, a 295-mile stretch of tracks from Chattanooga, Tennessee, to Meridian, Mississippi. That meant more industrial jobs within the city. The passing trains also meant bringing regular mail, freight shipments and passengers from the eastern United States. By the late 1880s, the Trussville area had a blast furnace in the heart of what would become the Cahaba Project and its first land company. General merchandise stores such as Norrell's and T.E. Glenn Department Store opened. Drugstores such as Sims Drug Store, Trussville Drug Store and, later, Haisten's Drug Store opened. Grocery and food stores, like Guy Self's grocery store, Morrison's and other small markets, were opened, as were cafés and small restaurants.

While this was transpiring, the invention of the automobile was well known, and its popularity was growing. With the automobile came the necessity of vehicle service stations, and Mabe's Garage and Thomas Stephens's stations were two of the first in Trussville. By the time the Cahaba Project homes were constructed in the late 1930s, Trussville possessed all the amenities for a simple yet growing community. The community grew and continues to grow its industrial and business base.

Industry

The industrial base in Trussville is stronger and more diverse than most people think. The Trussville Industrial Development Board, a nine-member group, promotes industrial expansion for economic growth and employment within the city's limits. The board is authorized to sell or lease property to industrial tenants.

The biggest industrial tenant in the city of Trussville is Amerex Corporation, the world's largest manufacturer of hand portable and wheeled extinguishers for commercial and industrial applications. Ned Paine founded Amerex Corporation in Trussville in 1971 and served for twenty years, from 1993 to 2003, on the Industrial Development Board. Paine retired from the company on September 30, 1999. Paine, who served also on the Jefferson County School Foundation, helped fund the facilities and establish a program for a technical education lab at Hewitt-Trussville Junior High School. In 1999, he and his wife, Goldie, donated thirty-one acres of property along U.S. Highway 11 near Amerex Corporation for what are now the campuses of Paine Primary School and Paine Intermediate School. He was chairman of the committee that determined it was feasible to start a Trussville school

The exterior of Amerex Corporation, a manufacturer of fire extinguishers. *Gary Lloyd.*

system and served as a charter member of the board of education in Trussville from 2004 to 2005. The Hewitt-Trussville High School softball field off Trussville-Clay Road is named in Goldie Paine's honor. Amerex Corporation still operates in Trussville, an affiliate of McWane Inc.

The McPherson Companies, one of the largest independent lubricant distributors in the United States, was founded in Oneonta, Alabama, in 1971 but now has its corporate offices in Trussville. Because of growth, McPherson moved to a larger distribution center from Oneonta to Trussville in 2001. Relocating to Trussville meant extensive rail car capacity to support the bulk oil needs and additional acreage for future expansion. In 2007, the McPherson Companies moved its corporate offices from Birmingham to Trussville, built adjacent to the regional distribution facility. Today, the McPherson Companies distributes around 16 million gallons of lubricant and is a full-service petroleum products and services company. The company was founded by Charles McPherson, and its president is now his eldest son, Ken McPherson.

Near these two titans of industry is a vacant building once occupied by Gold Kist Inc., a chicken-processing plant that closed in 2003. Gold Kist had its troubles in Trussville, largely due to its proximity to the Cahaba River. In 1993, Gold Kist was fined $19,000 for violating water pollution standards, according to the Alabama Department of Environmental Management. ADEM fined the plant for allowing too much of certain pollutants to enter an unnamed tributary of Little Cahaba Creek, which is a tributary of the Cahaba River. ADEM officials said at the time that Gold Kist violated discharge limits thirty-five times from June 1992 to July 1993. Four were for excess ammonia, eighteen were for total residual chlorine, three were for nitrogen, eight were for fecal coliform and two were for oil and grease. Gold Kist at the time designed and installed a new wastewater treatment system. Gold Kist in January 1999 asked ADEM to establish looser nitrogen limits during the winter months, part of the company's National Pollutant Discharge Elimination System renewal application. Trussville mayor Gene Melton, the Cahaba River Society and other groups spoke against the request, saying that it would stress the Cahaba River. Gold Kist argued that the limits were too stringent.

In early 2001, Gold Kist was fined $5,600 for water-quality violations. In response, the company announced that it would make $100,000 worth of improvements at the Trussville plant on Will Pond Road to stop the ongoing pollution of the tributary of the Cahaba River. At the time, seventy-seven miles of the Cahaba River were classified under the U.S. Clean Water Act as

The former Gold Kist chicken-processing plant on Will Pond Road. *Gary Lloyd.*

impaired by pollution from nutrients such as nitrogen. ADEM said that legal and illegal pollution from Gold Kist may have contributed to the nutrient problem, though fertilizers and treated sewage wastewater were also believed to have been at fault.

Gold Kist announced its closing of the Trussville plant in September 2003 as part of its attempt to consolidate operations in Alabama. The move cut about five hundred jobs. In 2005, the Trussville Industrial Development Board bought the Gold Kist property to expand the Trussville Industrial Park. Part of the property was then sold to McPherson Oil. The Trussville City Council in December 2012 authorized the city's purchase of the 53.27-acre site for $1.7 million. The property at that time was owned by Scottsman Trades, which was owned by McPherson Oil. The property had been valued at $4.5 million. The property includes 10,000 square feet of office space and 120,000 square feet of warehouse space, which could allow the city of Trussville to have an operations center in the future. The facility, located not far from Paine Primary School and Paine Intermediate School, could also securely house Trussville City Schools buses. In March 2013, the Trussville City Council approved of going out to bid on 3,000 feet of 6-foot-tall security fencing to install around the former chicken-processing plant.

Two main construction companies headquartered in Trussville are Bob Smith Construction and Blalock Building Company. Bob Smith Construction was incorporated in 1986 in Center Point, Alabama. In 1993, the company relocated to Tarrant, Alabama, but, in 1998 and 2005, moved to two offices in Trussville. The company handles design, budgeting, value engineering, new project construction and existing building repair and renovations. Blalock Building Company has offices on U.S. Highway 11 in

Trussville and, in the summer of 2013, was revealed as the low bidder to construct the new Hewitt-Trussville Stadium and Sports Complex, a high school football stadium with adjoining track and field capabilities near the Trussville Civic Center. The company bid $13,353,900 to build the stadium and accompanying soccer concessions and restroom building beside a soccer field in front of the Trussville Civic Center.

Steyr Arms Inc., a manufacturer of firearms, had been a lesser-known industry to Trussville residents until August 2013, when it was announced that the gun maker was moving its operations from Trussville to Bessemer, Alabama. A subsidiary of Austria-based Steyr Mannlicher, the company planned a $1.7 million expansion that would triple its workforce in Bessemer. Steyr Arms Inc. was set to complete its relocation by June 2014.

Another Trussville industry that was growing in 2013 was SPOC Automation Inc., a manufacturer of variable-frequency drive solutions for the oil and gas industry. The company in September 2013 completed its third production facility at its Trussville location on U.S. Highway 11. The company planned to add another facility early in 2014 that would house office space and a test facility.

In 2013, the Trussville Industrial Development Board was working to list the city's available properties on the Economic Development Partnership of Alabama website to be advertised. Properties at the Trussville Industrial Park are zoned for light industrial development. Some companies located there include Quality Machine Works, G.R. Manufacturing Inc. and Robinson Fans Service & Equipment Center, among others.

Business

Mabe Power and Equipment Center, prior to its closing in 2012, was the longest continuously operating business in the city of Trussville. With the invention of the automobile came service and mechanic stations in the early 1900s. Bill Mabe opened a garage where automobiles were serviced and repaired in Trussville in February 1921. A generator there also provided electricity for customers in Trussville for one dollar per month for each bulb. In the 1930s, the station was remodeled and operated as Bill Mabe's One Stop Service Station, when gasoline for automobiles cost motorists less than twenty cents per gallon. John Mabe, Bill's son, ran the station as well, which eventually became known as Mabe Garage

Mabe's Garage, run by Bill Mabe, in the mid-1900s. *Kathy Kennedy.*

and Lawnmower Repair. That name was changed to Mabe Power and Equipment Center in 1990 because the business was no longer servicing and repairing automobiles, only lawn equipment, such as lawnmowers, weed trimmers and chainsaws. Kathy Mabe Kennedy, John's daughter, owned the business from 2007 to its close on April 30, 2012, a decision based on family reasons, a 2003 flood that caused extensive damage to the Main Street business district and three consecutive years of drought. At the time of its closing, the Mabe business had been open for ninety-one years and run by three generations of Mabes. Late in 2013, the large Main Street property was still up for sale.

The business climate in Trussville has grown seemingly every year since the 1980s, prior to that acting as a bedroom community with mainly just the essential businesses—service stations, drugstores, department stores, markets and cafés. Before the huge influx in Trussville's population in the 1990s, the commercial opportunities in Trussville were relatively minimal compared with other Birmingham-area cities. Vehicles could be purchased at Trussville Motors on Main Street, right next to the Trussville Municipal Building. Across the street from that was the Dairy Cone, an ice cream shop that was a popular hangout. A lot of the small-town charm that the city of Trussville once possessed is gone, taken by developments. Trussville has become one of the most popular places to open a business, given its proximity to interstates and an increasing population. Over the past twenty or so years, the city has seen a big rise in commercial development, especially in the categories of retail and restaurants.

Retail

Trussville seemingly has something for everyone these days. The Trussville Crossings shopping center on Chalkville Mountain Road opened in 2000 and included a Walmart Super Center. Walmart is the anchor in this area and is surrounded by a nearby K-Mart, Sam's Club, Kohl's, Hibbett Sports and Marshalls. Later in 2000, the two anchor stores at the Colonial Promenade at Tutwiler Farm, Super Target and the Home Depot, opened. Other retail stores in this center include Academy Sports & Outdoors, Old Navy, Books-A-Million, Bed Bath & Beyond, T.J. Maxx and Michaels. Six years later, the Pinnacle at Tutwiler Farm opened behind the Colonial Promenade at Tutwiler Farm. Retail businesses at this center are two Belk stores, JCPenney, hhgregg, Best Buy, American Eagle, Aéropostale, Bama Fever/Tiger Pride, Buckle, Chico's, Foot Locker, Kay Jewelers, Haverty's, Kirkland's Home and others.

The Trussville Crossings shopping center on Chalkville Mountain Road, anchored by Walmart. *Gary Lloyd.*

The Colonial Promenade at Tutwiler Farm shopping center on U.S. Highway 11. *Gary Lloyd.*

For all the big-name stores that are scattered along U.S. Highway 11 and Chalkville Mountain Road, Trussville also has the smaller family-owned stores, the types of retail businesses that give a city a certain level of uniqueness. Most of these stores are located in the downtown area of Trussville, on or near Main Street. The most well known, outside the former Mabe business, is Braden's Furniture, located at the corner of Main Street and North Chalkville Road. The furniture store was founded in 1956 by Vernon and Kathleen Braden. In 1974, their son, Billy Braden, joined the company and married Teresa, with whom he has four children and three grandchildren. Billy Braden bought the company from his father in 1989 and doubled the store's size. The store in late 2013 was still operating in this location, a fixture on Main Street to some of the oldest Trussville residents. The future of Braden's Furniture in that location was in question, though, because a project to construct a dedicated right turn lane from Vann Circle to Main Street along North Chalkville Road was in full effect late in 2013. The Trussville City Council in October 2013 authorized Mayor Gene Melton to close on the Ellison Investments property, located between the Braden's Furniture buildings, for a future right turn lane. Billy Braden said his business's property likely appraises for well in excess of $1 million. The right turn lane was expected to be in place by 2016. Braden said his first choice was to relocate the furniture business to somewhere in downtown Trussville.

Other Trussville businesses with a bit of local touch include Barnett Furniture, the Sassy Sofa, Gigi's Boutique, the Spotted Zebra, the Straw Hat,

Vernon Braden, the former owner of Braden's Furniture, drives baseball players in a parade during the late 1950s or early 1960s. *Braden's Furniture.*

Southern Magnolia, Mary's Boutique, the Frequent Flower and more. The city of Trussville has done a good job of preserving its downtown and of not allowing big-box stores and chains to take over. Retail is aplenty throughout Trussville, yet the heart of the city still maintains a small-town feel.

Restaurants

There is no shortage of restaurants from which to choose in Trussville. There are close to one hundred eateries—fast food and dine-in—that serve the immediate Trussville area. Most of the small cafés and family-owned restaurants are gone, though some are still open and flourishing in the downtown area. One of the most popular Main Street restaurants is Joel's Restaurant, which opened in 1983. Owned and operated by Joel and Peggy Rickles, the restaurant offers a daily selection of meats, vegetables, homemade desserts and sweet tea. Golden Rule Bar-B-Q is another mainstay in Trussville, located on South Chalkville Road by the railroad tracks just above the banks of Pinchgut Creek. Many who work in downtown Trussville choose Golden Rule Bar-B-Q for lunch, as do train operators who have stops in the Trussville area. Café on Main is a small restaurant that opened on Main Street on August 12, 2000. Mostly open during lunch hours, Café on Main serves daily meats and vegetables. There is also a Café on Main in Oneonta, Alabama. The Chocolate Biscuit is a tearoom on Main Street that is popular for hosting bridal luncheons and baby showers. The Three Earred Rabbit on Main Street provides a look into the past, operating as an old-fashioned soda fountain and bakery. The food is made to order, and the business also offers bakery goods and gift baskets.

Outside the immediate downtown district, however, there are many chain dine-in restaurants and fast food establishments. Most of the longest-operating restaurants opened when the two large shopping centers were completed in the late 1990s and early 2000s. In the Chalkville Mountain Road area, fast food restaurants include Taco Bell, Wendy's, McDonald's, Arby's, Burger King, Chick-fil-A, Dairy Queen, Krystal, Little Caesar's, Papa John's, Pizza Hut, Milo's, Paul's Hot Dogs, Subway, What-A-Burger and Zaxby's. More sit-down type restaurants in this area of Trussville include Applebee's, Buffalo Wild Wings, Costa's Mediterranean, Cracker Barrel, East Buffet, Frontera Grill, Konomi, Trios, Lone Star Steakhouse, Waffle House, Ruby Tuesday, Palace, Seafood & Chicken Box, Sherry's Café and the Southern Diner.

The U.S. Highway 11 area has seen more development over the past fifteen or so years than the Chalkville Mountain Road side of the city. Fast food restaurants throughout the U.S. Highway 11 corridor are Arby's, Burger King, Jack's, Kentucky Fried Chicken, McDonald's, Zaxby's and Wendy's. More small to family-sized restaurants exist in this area as there are also more diverse shopping opportunities. Dine-in establishments include Cajun Steamer, Chili's Bar and Grill, Firehouse Subs, Mizu Japanese Steakhouse, Five Guys Burgers & Fries, Habanero's Mexican Grill, Jim 'N Nick's, La Bamba Mexican Grill Cantina, Lee Gardens, Logan's Roadhouse, Olive Garden, Red Lobster, Red Robin and Rock 'N' Roll Sushi. Other restaurants that opened in the last few years include Salvatore's Pizza, Tortugas, Parish Seafood & Oyster House, Dunkin' Donuts, Taziki's Mediterranean Café and Bojangles. More restaurants are expected to potentially locate in Trussville soon, both family restaurants and fast food businesses.

Other Amenities

Trussville is more than retail and restaurants, and the city's large residential base and proximity to interstates help in attracting other businesses. There are six hotels that are in or near Trussville and a couple car dealerships.

For the kids, two businesses stand out. PlayStation, a skating rink that also provides arcade games, batting cages, laser tag, mini golf and a go-kart track, opened on Watterson Curve near Trussville's U.S. Post Office in 1996. The Carter family, who have much experience in the business, own the skating rink. Ruth and J.P. Carter owned skating rinks dating back to 1959, opening rinks in Gadsden, Anniston, Roebuck, Birmingham, Gardendale, Hoover and Irondale. The skating rink is still open in Trussville, catering mostly to children and young teenagers.

Lightning Strikes is a bowling alley that opened in the early 2000s on Roosevelt Boulevard between the Colonial Promenade at Tutwiler Farm and the Pinnacle at Tutwiler Farm shopping centers. The bowling alley was popular for people of all ages and, on multiple occasions, has been the site of nationally ESPN-televised Professional Bowling Association tournaments. The most recent professional event was held in the spring of 2013. Four-time PBA50 Player of the Year Tom Baker won the PBA50 Greater Birmingham Open, which included some of the most well-known bowlers in the country. In October 2013, Lightning Strikes was acquired for $2.1 million by Vermont-based Bowl New England Inc., which owns and operates about twenty bowling alleys in the Northeast; two in Chattanooga, Tennessee; and a couple more in North Carolina. Renamed Spare Time Entertainment, a two-phase renovation began in late 2013, which included removing eight lanes to add a two-level laser tag arena, adding a fifty- or seventy-five-piece arcade room and completely renovating the interior to include new seating, a new control desk, a restaurant and sports bar and a VIP suite with six to eight lanes. At the time of this writing, all renovations are expected to be completed by September 1, 2014.

Other fun amenities exist in the city of Trussville, as do small niche restaurants and shops. This trend of adding retail stores, restaurants and entertainment venues is expected to continue as Trussville grows. A key focus is on downtown Trussville.

Moving Main Street Forward

In the fall of 2010, the Food World grocery store on Main Street permanently closed. In 2011, America's Thrift Stores signed a fifteen-year lease on the building, something it could do without Trussville City Council approval since the city did not own the property. In October 2011, the city council approved a $750,000 loan to the city's Downtown Redevelopment Authority to assume the lease of the building, make necessary renovations and buy out the lease of America's Thrift Stores. City officials did not like that they had been unaware of the thrift store's buying the space, and most said that the business did not fit into Trussville's downtown master plan. Trussville paid the thrift store $250,000 to end its lease and paid about $22,000 per month in rent from October 2011 until late summer of 2013. In August 2013, the city council approved incentives and leases for Fresh Value Marketplace and 24e Fitness to occupy the former Food World, much to the delight of city officials and disapproval of area fitness center owners. As part of the approval, the city spent $912,000 to divide the building into two spaces and abated $800,000 in sales tax over a four-year period as an incentive for Fresh Value Marketplace.

After settling that downtown issue, the Trussville Planning and Zoning Board in October 2013 approved a new downtown master plan and recommended that the city council amend the city's zoning ordinance for downtown development and the sign ordinance to include regulations for the downtown district. The master plan's implementation included flood mitigation projects, traffic and streetscape improvements, a public shared parking system, business support and recruitment and downtown zoning and design standards. The plan's goals were to eventually make it easier to get around town; concentrate shopping, dining and cultural experiences; mitigate flooding problems that have persisted in the downtown area; and implement a design for a consistent, safe and attractive downtown. The plan approved extends from Kay Avenue on the west side of downtown to the Cahaba River on the east side. It also extends north of Main Street to Hewitt Street and down to the railroad tracks on the south side. The plan also included long-term goals of more green spaces, walkways and bicycle paths to create something of a village feel on Main Street.

A key component in creating this feel over time is alleviating traffic congestion. Knowing a redesign of downtown was coming, the city council in December 2011 approved preliminary engineering to be done for a widening of North Chalkville Road between First Baptist Church of Trussville and Main Street. To widen the road for a dedicated right turn lane, a few properties had to be acquired by the city. The city had hoped the federal government would help with the cost, but it declined due to the area's historic nature. In October 2013, Mayor Gene Melton predicted that acquiring all the necessary properties to construct the right turn lane could cost about $2.2 million. Part of the project also included properly aligning Linden Street with the road that leads to the Trussville City Schools Central Office.

The fruits of the downtown master plan project remain to be seen, as the entire revitalization period is projected to be twenty to thirty years. However, if the goals are met, traffic is smoothed out and parking is made easy, residents will appreciate and often visit downtown Trussville, which is what potential businesses want to see. The current business climate in Trussville is strong, but the outlook for business in the future, especially in the downtown district, appears to be even stronger.

Chapter 9
CITY LANDMARKS

Trussville is home to many significant landmarks, both natural and man-made. The blending of older, more historic landmarks with newer, more modern ones makes for diverse interests in the city, a big reason why it is such a desired city to call home.

The Cahaba River and Civitan Park

The Cahaba River is the longest free-flowing river in the state of Alabama, one of the most scenic and biologically diverse rivers in the country. The 194-mile river passes through Trussville and eventually joins with the Alabama River in Dallas County. The river supports more than 60 rare and endangered plant and animal species, some of which are found nowhere else in the world. More than 130 species of fish are found in the Cahaba River. The river provides fishing, swimming and tubing opportunities in Trussville and neighboring cities. The Cahaba River Society, whose mission is to restore and protect the river's watershed and diversity, serves the Birmingham metro area and is very active in Trussville. Founded as a nonprofit organization in 1988, the Cahaba River Society employs a range of education, collaboration and policy advocacy. As the Cahaba River is the main drinking water source for the Birmingham Water Works Board, which serves almost one-fifth of the state's population, it is important for the society to help strengthen water resource protection policies at the state level. The Cahaba River Society's primary fundraiser, the Cahaba River Fry-Down, has been held each year in Trussville since 2010. The event, which features a fish-frying competition and other activities, seeks to educate attendees through water-smart learning activities. Children and adults explore the relationship among water quality, habitat, drinking water and the health of aquatic life, humans and wildlife.

The most recognizable Trussville landmark associated with the Cahaba River is the Civitan Bridge, located in downtown Trussville's Civitan Park. The bridge was constructed in Argo in 1901, dismantled and moved to Ketona and then dismantled again and moved to Happy Hollow Road in 1940. With a new bridge and road built for the Happy Hollow area, the bridge was determined to be useless and was subsequently abandoned. The Trussville Civitan Club stepped in, spearheading a project that transported the bridge to its present location in Civitan Park. The club's project rallied support throughout the city, attracting private citizens, civic organizations and businesses to help in the cause. Citizens donated money to purchase two hundred wooden planks necessary to floor the bridge. Businesses worked to relocate the bridge, prepare the site and sandblast and paint the structure green. A metal plate bearing the name of the donor is installed on each plank on the bridge. At the bridge's dedication ceremony, a plaque was presented that officially designated the bridge as a historic site in Jefferson County. The Trussville Chamber of Commerce nominated the bridge project for consideration in the U.S. Department of Interior's National "Take Pride in America" awards program. The Trussville Civitan Club was awarded a Certificate of Merit at a ceremony in Washington, D.C. That certificate hangs in the Trussville Area Chamber of Commerce's headquarters at Heritage Hall on Parkway Drive. The footbridge is easily visible from U.S. Highway 11 and serves people who wish to access both banks of the Cahaba River below.

A greenways project began in 1998 to enhance the Cahaba River and parks throughout Trussville. The project, still unfinished in 2013, was to include a lighted walking trail that would stretch from Civitan Park to the Trussville Sports Complex, running parallel to the river the whole way. The $2.2 million project is federally funded through a grant and administered by the Alabama Department of Transportation. The city of Trussville has had no supervisory authority over any contractor working on the project. State officials halted work on a portion of the project in September 2012 when one man said he believed that there were archaeological artifacts on the construction site. The concern closed a nearby Frisbee disc golf course until it was determined that there were no artifacts. The course was reopened in March 2013. Real problems with the greenways project began the next month, when the Alabama Department of Environmental Management notified the city of Trussville in writing of concerns it had with the project, including soil erosion, improperly kept silt fences and barren land that was not seeded or covered with hay to prevent runoff. City officials at the time expressed

The Veterans Memorial Monument in Civitan Park was unfinished in 2013. *Gary Lloyd.*

their displeasure with the project's contractor, which by May 2013 had fewer than thirty workdays to complete the project before entering into a liquidated damages penalty, which would have included the contractor owing the Alabama Department of Transportation large sums of money. The contractor had begun the project in April 2012. In late May 2013, to make the project compliant with the Alabama Department of Environmental Management, Cahaba Disaster Recovery assisted the Alabama Department of Transportation, most notably helping to spread about 768 bales of hay around the Cahaba River at Civitan Park. The Trussville City Council agreed to pay Cahaba Disaster Recovery up to $25,000.00 for the work it had done, and the project was then determined to be compliant with the environmental management department standards. The city council in June 2013 approved of spending $16,109.72 for the purchase and installation of 3,850 feet of 6-foot-high fencing with five 12-foot gates to circle Civitan Park. The fencing was purchased to act as security while the greenways were completed. Later that month, it was announced that the contractor who had been charged with completing the project was pulled off the job and that the Alabama Department of Transportation was seeking a replacement. Trussville Parks and Recreation Department crews were allowed into the park to cut grass that had grown tall and to clean up. As of this writing, the project is expected to be completed sometime in 2014.

Another aspect of Civitan Park is the Veterans' Memorial Monument, announced as a new project in 2010. The idea for the memorial came from longtime Trussville Historical Society member Venie Payne, whose husband, H.B. Payne, served in World War II as a sergeant in the 276th Combat Engineers. He was wounded in combat on the Bridge at Remagen and was discharged in 1945. He later received the Presidential Unit Citation and Purple Heart. His service prompted Venie Payne to create the memorial monument. The thirty-foot tower was completely erected in late 2011, though names and other historical milestones were still being added to it in 2012 and 2013, after Venie Payne's death. When complete, the memorial will include names and dates of service for close to two hundred local veterans.

Camp Gertrude Coleman

The Girl Scouts was founded in 1912 by Juliette Gordon Low, and ten years later, local troops began to emerge in Jefferson County, Alabama. On May 22, 1925, the Girl Scouts of Jefferson County incorporated for the express

Girl Scouts eat snacks and drink milk at Camp Gertrude Coleman in 1939. *Sarah Edwards.*

purpose of buying land to establish a camp. That land was located on the more northeastern side of the city, along a stretch of the Cahaba River. To get the $1,000 down payment necessary to purchase the land, Girl Scouts of Jefferson County treasurer Winifred Collins obtained a promise of $500 if she could raise the rest of the funds in Birmingham. Gordon Crawford, Tennessee Coal and Iron's director in Birmingham and a relative of Juliette Gordon Low, gave the first $300. Collins raised the remaining funds from other local businessmen in Birmingham.

The camp opened in 1925 under the name Camp Gertrude Coleman, named after its first commissioner, who died six months prior to its opening. The first trustees were Mrs. Herbert C. Stockham, the daughter-in-law of the founder of Stockham Pipe and Valve; Mrs. W.C. Bonham; and Winifred Collins. John Shields Coleman, Gertrude Coleman's husband, a lawyer who later became director of the Birmingham branch of the Federal Reserve Bank of Atlanta, prepared the documents for the purchase of the land.

Camp Gertrude Coleman has much history as the third-longest-operating Girl Scouts camp in the United States and the longest continuously operating Girl Scouts camp in the state of Alabama. The camp even remained open during the Great Depression and World War II because of the dedication of its attendees. Most camps closed during this time so that their leaders could contribute to the war effort.

It was the state's first fully integrated camp. Camp Gertrude Coleman consists of thirty-four wooden structures and outbuildings constructed between 1925 and 1994. The director's cabin was built in 1925 and is the oldest structure at the camp, which is situated on about 140 acres of land along the Cahaba River. Thousands of girls and women—a couple of generations of mothers and daughters, even—have spent summers and weekends at Camp Gertrude Coleman, learning about the Cahaba River's biodiversity, about sweet gum and big-leaf magnolia trees how to canoe and make campfires, among other things.

Under the leadership of the Girl Scouts of Cahaba Council for years, the Girl Scouts of North-Central Alabama was chartered on November 1, 2007, as a result of a merger of the Cahaba Council, the Tombigbee Girl Scout Council, Girl Scouts of North Alabama and the Cottaquilla Girl Scout Council. The Girl Scouts of North-Central Alabama serves thirty-six of the state's sixty-seven counties.

The eighty-nine years of continuous operation of Camp Gertrude Coleman was threatened on May 9, 2012, when the Girl Scouts of North-Central Alabama Board of Directors voted to approve a three-phase property plan, which included closing and divesting Camp Gertrude Coleman, Camp Anderel in Rogersville, Camp Tombigbee in Greene County and Camp Trico in Guntersville. The plan was the result of significant operating losses in 2011. As part of the plan, Camp Anderel and Camp Tombigbee would permanently closed on August 31, 2012, while Camp Coleman and Camp Trico would permanently close on May 31, 2013. At the approval of divesting Camp Gertrude Coleman, concerns were expressed that there could be a loss of donors with the sale of the camp. With the approval of divesting four camps came the approval to expand the resident camp, programs and activities at the Kanawahala Program Center in Chelsea and Camp Cottaquilla in Anniston.

On the day the Girl Scouts of North-Central Alabama Board of Directors voted in favor of the three-phase property plan, a group of Girl Scouts alumnae gathered in a living room and formed Friends of Camp Coleman, a group whose goal was to preserve Camp Gertrude Coleman and its outdoor opportunities in order to build girls of courage, confidence and character. On July 16, 2012, the group became a 501c3 nonprofit organization committed

The director's cabin at Camp Gertrude Coleman is the oldest structure at the 140-acre campsite. *Gary Lloyd.*

to saving Camp Gertrude Coleman and establishing an endowment fund to ensure that Girl Scouts would be able to continue going to Camp Gertrude Coleman for its recreation opportunities.

In March 2013, Trussville mayor Gene Melton offered for the city of Trussville to buy the camp for $700,000. The 140-acre site had been appraised for about $2.1 million. Melton wanted the camp to remain a protected green space in Trussville and for Girl Scouts to continue to use the property. The Girl Scouts of North-Central Alabama rejected his offer. There were around 250 Girl Scouts in the Trussville area in early 2013.

In May 2013, a historical marker was unveiled at Camp Gertrude Coleman, a sign of being favorably reviewed by the Alabama Historical Commission to be listed on the Alabama Register of Landmarks and Heritage. The marker says that it was dedicated "in remembrance of all of the courageous women who established this site and those who sustained it over the years so that girls could enjoy the benefits of camping envisioned by Juliette Low." A letter from the Alabama Historical Commission stated that landmarks listed on the historical register are worthy of both recognition and preservation.

On May 29, 2013, two days before Camp Coleman was set to be permanently closed, the Girl Scouts of North-Central Alabama Board of Directors approved an amendment to the three-phase property plan, choosing to rest Camp Gertrude Coleman and Camp Trico while the new board of directors, which was elected a month prior, further evaluated the three-phase property plan. The approval ensured that Camp Coleman would continue to be the longest continuously operating Girl Scouts camp in the state. Two days after the amendment was approved, the day the camp would have closed permanently, a group of Girl Scouts, experienced and young, were at Camp Gertrude Coleman. Confidence and hope were their prevailing emotions as they looked forward to a definitive reopening of the camp in the future. A major step in that direction was achieved less than two weeks later.

On June 12, 2013, the Girl Scouts of North-Central Alabama Board of Directors unanimously voted in favor of a resolution to reconsider the three-phase property plan. The resolution stated that no camp properties would be sold during the reevaluation process, pending the outcome of a new, comprehensive strategic plan that would be developed. That plan was to include input from the Girl Scouts membership, outside experts and community partners. The board of directors and Friends of Camp Coleman spent the better part of 2013 holding brainstorming meetings to determine their next steps. With the resting of Camp Gertrude Coleman, the Trussville City Council in July 2013 approved a resolution to remove the stop sign on North Lake Drive at the entrance to the camp. The resting of the camp reduced the amount of traffic through the adjoining neighborhood and negated the need for stop signs on North Lake Drive at the camp's entrance. On November 2, 2013, a work party volunteer event for the Girl Scouts was held at Camp Gertrude Coleman, a day to clean up to help maintain the camp's beauty.

On November 20, 2013, the Girl Scouts of North-Central Alabama Board of Directors unanimously passed a resolution that allowed the closed and rested camps, including Camp Gertrude Coleman, to be open on a limited-use basis for troop camping beginning in January 2014. The camps were to remain open pending the outcome of the reevaluation and strategic planning process. Limited use meant that no staff, instructors or services would be provided and that troops would be responsible for bringing their own equipment and supplies. At the time of this announcement, which was met with joy and optimism from Girl Scouts members, Sarah Edwards, the board of directors president who had been instrumental in the development of the Friends of Camp Coleman, said that since the three-phase property plan had been approved, a number of members had stepped forward with creative ideas and solutions that would allow the camps to reopen on a limited-use basis. Edwards said that the board of directors was ultimately responsible for the fiduciary management of the Girl Scouts of North-Central Alabama and recognized the importance of ensuring that the reopening of the camps was done so with a lot of thought.

The permanent future of Camp Gertrude Coleman remains to be seen in early 2014.

The Mall

The Mall is in the center of the Cahaba Project in Trussville. This area was designed to resemble the National Mall in Washington, D.C., with the historic school building on Parkway Drive in the background. The Mall is the location of outdoor city events, such as Trussville City Fest in May, which for thirty-two years prior to 2013 was known as Dog Daze and was held each August. The west side of the Mall is where the city's Christmas tree stands, lit every December as part of the annual Christmas parade, which passes through the Mall area. The Mall also hosts a fireworks show every July 4, farmers' markets and recreational sports and is a popular route for Hewitt-Trussville High School's homecoming parades.

Heritage Hall

Just beyond the east side of the Mall beside the New Deal–era school building is Heritage Hall, originally a retail general store and filling station managed by the Cahaba Cooperative Association. Built in 1938 along with the homes in the Cahaba Project, the store served the needs of the Cahaba Project residents. In 1951, four years after Trussville incorporated as a town, the town bought the general store to establish a community center and library. It later served as band and choral rooms for the high school.

In 1988, on the building's fiftieth anniversary, the Trussville Industrial Development Board restored the building. The building was dedicated to the preservation and development of the historic, civic and cultural heritage of the city through the Trussville Historical Board, the Trussville Chamber of Commerce and the Arts Council of the Trussville Area. Members of that board were Clarence Boatwright, Vernon Braden, Don Haisten, Woodrow Hayden, David Nicodemus, David Richardson, Kenneth Scott and Bill Vann. The Trussville Chamber of Commerce had existed since 1946 but did not have a permanent office until the store's restoration in 1988. Now known as the Trussville Area Chamber of Commerce, the chamber office is still located in a section of Heritage Hall and promotes the local business community. The left side of Heritage Hall holds old yearbooks, newspaper articles, books, artifacts, photos and other historical findings relative to the city of Trussville. The backside of Heritage Hall, near the Trussville City Pool, is ACTA Theatre, where local students and residents participate in dramas, comedies and musicals. The community theater typically features a winter, spring, fall and Christmas show each year.

Jack Wood Stadium and Hewitt-Trussville Stadium

The football stadium is another highly visible landmark in the Cahaba Project, sitting just beside the school building on Parkway Drive. A locker room, weight room and school classrooms were located under the home side bleachers. The land for the Hewitt-Trussville Stadium was deeded to Jefferson County by the City of Trussville. The city constructed the football field, fence and lighting at an approximate cost of $20,000 in the late 1940s. Built with an original capacity of 3,500 people, the stadium was dedicated and used for the first time on September 16, 1949. The Hewitt-Trussville High School football team posted a 3-7 record in its first season there in 1949, winning the September 16 game 25–6 over Mortimer Jordan. Jim Owens coached the Hewitt-Trussville football team for its first two seasons in the stadium, compiling an overall record of 7-11-1. Oren Prentice "Piggy" Mitchell led the football program from 1951 until 1963, coaching the Huskies to a 61-46-7 record. Geddes Self Jr. was the head coach in 1965 and 1966, posting a 5-15 record. Herbert Eubanks led the Hewitt-Trussville program from 1968 to 1971. He had an overall record of 12-25-1, with nine of his wins coming at the home stadium. Morris Higginbotham was the next coach to roam the Hewitt-Trussville Stadium sidelines, coaching the Huskies

Jack Wood Stadium has hosted high school football games in Trussville since 1949. *Gary Lloyd.*

to a 24-14-1 record between 1972 and 1975. Chip Stewart was the head coach from 1976 to 1982, compiling a 17-48-1 mark. With little success in the late 1970s and early 1980s, Jack Wood was brought in as the new Hewitt-Trussville head football coach in 1983, making him one of the youngest head coaches in the state of Alabama. Despite a record of 13-20 in his first three seasons, Wood coached Hewitt-Trussville to a 128-58 record between 1986 and 2001, finishing with an overall losing record just twice in that span. In 1992, Hewitt-Trussville won a school-record twelve games, including six shutout victories, before losing 14–0 to Lee Montgomery in the school's only state championship appearance. Wood was honored as the Alabama Sports Writers Association's top coach that season. In 1998, the football stadium was renamed Jack Wood Stadium in his honor. Wood retired from coaching after the 2001 season and, in 2003, was inducted into the Alabama High School Athletic Association Hall of Fame.

Wood's coaching replacement was Hal Riddle, a former Hewitt-Trussville quarterback who had been the head coach at Erwin, Mortimer Jordan and nearby Clay-Chalkville. He had also been an assistant coach under Wood at Hewitt-Trussville. In Riddle's first season at Clay-Chalkville in 1999, the Cougars posted a 12-3 record and beat Lee Montgomery 30–27 to win the program's only football state championship. Riddle has been the Hewitt-

Trussville head coach since 2002, leading the program to a 79-55 record through the 2013 high school football season. As of this writing, he has compiled seven winning seasons since 2002 at Hewitt-Trussville.

In 2012, it was determined that Jack Wood Stadium had too many deficiencies to continue on as Hewitt-Trussville's high school football stadium. The stadium's infrastructure was failing and the amount of restrooms did not meet state standards for a Class 6A school, the largest classification in Alabama. The grassy area behind the Trussville Civic Center, which used to be a dairy farm and was identified in 1992 as a possible place for historical registration, was chosen as the site for the new Hewitt-Trussville Stadium.

The site chosen for the new stadium sat close to the Cahaba River, leading University of Alabama archaeological researchers to believe that the area was likely settled by tribes between 500 and 1000 BC and AD 600 and 1000. Researchers believed the reason the area was chosen for settlement had to do with populations moving across landscapes. It is known that the West Jefferson phase occupants of the Black Warrior Valley began moving eastward into the Cahaba and Coosa Valleys about 1,200 years ago. They brought new pottery vessel technology, subsistence strategies and lithic tools, some of which were made of raw materials from the Black Warrior Valley that they likely brought with them or traded for, researchers said. Two areas of the stadium site were called into question. The higher elevated area was believed to have been flooded by the river, and the lower site was used when the river's banks were much lower. The areas were likely used as resource-gathering areas at a time when groups of people were generally nomadic hunter-gatherers, finding vegetables and fruit rather than planting them. The area was an occasional seasonal base settlement, researchers hypothesized. While combing the area for artifacts as part of an archaeological dig in the summer of 2013, University of Alabama researchers discovered a large, finely serrated spear point and a piece of pottery featuring rectangular designs generally found in the Tombigbee region. An oven, living surface, stone-made tools and many other man-made pottery pieces were found during the dig, which cost the City of Trussville $142,577.24. The dig was completed in August 2013, and the U.S. Army Corps of Engineers later signed off on the stadium project to move forward. Artifacts gathered were sent to be analyzed in Moundville, Alabama, near Tuscaloosa. Specialized samples were sent off for dating, botanical analysis and geoarchaeological studies, information that was to be included in the University of Alabama Office of Archaeological Research's final report on the site of the new stadium. Through starch analysis of artifacts, researchers said they would be

Many projectile points and man-made pottery pieces were found during an archaeological dig at the Hewitt-Trussville Stadium site. *Gary Lloyd.*

able to determine how old their findings were, what the natives were using to harvest food and animals, what resources were being used and how they were using the landscape.

Trussville-based Blalock Building Company won the bid to build Hewitt-Trussville Stadium with a bid of $14,626,550 in June 2013. The base bid was $13,353,900, but alternates of precast concrete visitor seating, a multipurpose field lighting package, overflow parking, a kitchen equipment upgrade for the visitor concession, precast concrete for a home side and visitor side expansion and a soccer concessions and restroom building raised the base price. Part of the project included the construction of a large, three-lane bridge over the Cahaba River, connecting Hewitt-Trussville High School to the stadium area. In July 2013, the building company was officially approved as the contractor for the stadium project.

The company Brasfield & Gorrie won the bid for the Husky Parkway bridge project with a base bid of $3,281,445.13. The bridge was to be built with a pedestrian lane and would cover more than three hundred feet. City officials said at the time that the bridge would provide additional safety

Construction of the new Hewitt-Trussville Stadium and Husky Parkway bridge was underway in 2013 near the Trussville Civic Center (background). *Ron Burkett.*

measures for students who had to drive on Deerfoot Parkway and Trussville-Clay Road to get to the football practice fields and field house adjacent to the new stadium site.

Ground was broken at the Hewitt-Trussville Stadium site on September 25, 2013, signifying the start of construction. City of Trussville and Trussville City Schools officials, as well as Blalock Building Company employees, wore white hard hats and moved the first dirt with gold-bladed shovels. Construction of the new stadium began almost immediately afterward, and as of this writing, the new stadium is expected to open for high school football play in late September 2014. With its completion, the plan is for Jack Wood Stadium to be torn down and its area used as a community park with a smaller walking track.

Historic Homes

The Cahaba Project is what most Trussville residents think of when they think of historic homes in the city. But there are others. Just beyond the

Cahaba Project on North Chalkville Road is the Hickman-Yarbrough house, believed to have been built in the 1850s. Built on property owned by John Truss, the original home is believed to have burned down after William Peyton Hickman purchased it. Hickman was the builder of the current house that stands today. Hickman was a businessman, merchant and treasurer in Jefferson County. At one time, Hickman owned nearly three thousand acres around the house. The Hickman-Yarbrough house is listed as a historical home in Jefferson County, originally built with a mansard roof. There were originally four bedrooms and an upstairs landing. Around the 1920s, the mansard roof was changed to a hip roof. Today, the house includes two bedrooms, one office and one upstairs bathroom. The house has undergone many changes over the years. Six of the ten fireplaces were converted into coal fireplaces, and today, there are electric logs in all but one of them. The kitchen fireplace has ventless gas logs in it. The kitchen was initially located where a pergola stands on the upper patio, and the current laundry room was the house's slaves' bedroom years ago. On the lower side of the house is a mountain stone, where it is believed that ladies would climb into the horse buggies or mount their horses. Pins to tie horses' reins to are still in the stone wall. A few pickets of the fence built in 1910 have been replaced due to deterioration. Dave and Joni Parrish purchased the Hickman-Yarbrough house in 1998 and still live there today, calling the home a labor of love.

The Elliot House is another historic Trussville home, added to the Alabama Register of Landmarks and Heritage by the Alabama Historical Commission in 2008. The home was built around 1889 by a section foreman of the Louisville and Nashville Railroad. When added to the register, the Elliot House retained many of its original features, including fireplaces, basic U-shape and outbuildings.

The Edwards House was also constructed in the late 1800s, a two-story frame building supported by rock piers. The last members of the Edwards family to live in the house were George and Mary Edwards. By 1989, the house and land belonged to W.S. Dinken Jr. The house was not open for public viewing in 1989.

Georgiana Davis Masonic Lodge No. 338

The Georgiana Davis Masonic Lodge No. 338 is located on Beechnut Street in Trussville, not far from Pinchgut Creek and Main Street. The

Sinkler Lathem's grave is located in Mt. Nebo Cemetery. Lathem deeded a plot of land to the Georgiana Davis Masonic Lodge for one dollar in 1868. *Gary Lloyd.*

lodge was recommended by Springville Lodge No. 280 on May 17, 1867. Springville Lodge is known as the Mother Lodge of the lodge at Trussville. Dispensation was granted to Georgiana Davis Masonic Lodge on July 2, 1867, by Grand Master Wilson Williams. The charter was granted on December 6, 1867, the first membership including nineteen men. The name Georgiana Davis was chosen because the first building used as a meeting place was a log cabin west of Trussville on the property belonging to Georgiana Davis, the widow of Dr. Elias Davis. The name was adopted for the lodge in honor of Dr. Davis and his family, and as a token of their respect for Georgiana.

On April 1, 1868, a plot of land was deeded to the lodge for $1 by Sinkler Lathem. On the same day and for an equal price, he deeded an equal and adjoining plot of land to Mt. Nebo Presbyterian Church. The deeds stipulated that the land was to be used for a Masonic lodge or church building, or else the land would revert back to the owner. Georgiana Davis Masonic Lodge and Mt. Nebo Presbyterian Church then built a frame house for $175 to be jointly occupied. The house was used until its demolition in 1899. The lodge and church then built a new building, in which the lodge met on the second floor.

In the early 1900s, the lodge meetings were held in the upstairs of D.N. Talley's department store on the corner of Main Street and Chalkville Road. The lodge hall present today on Beechnut Street was constructed in 1947, and the first meeting was held there was on August 21, 1948, when the Pinson Division of the Jefferson County Masonic Conference held its regular quarterly meeting. The first time Georgiana Davis Masonic Lodge members met there was on August 23, 1948. The mortgage on the building was paid off in April 1958, and a meeting was held on September 26, 1958, for the purpose of burning the mortgage. As the oldest member, Floyd Bradford performed the mortgage burning ceremony.

On November 17, 1971, Paul E. Bradford was elected Most Worshipful Grand Master for the year 1971–72, and three days later, the Georgiana Davis Masonic Lodge celebrated Paul E. Bradford Day in his honor. The celebration was held at Mason's Park in Trussville, and the featured speaker was Brother L. Leon Hearn, the former Grand Orator of the Grand Lodge of Alabama. Bradford was presented with a new Buick automobile from the Masons of Jefferson County and Springville Lodge No. 280 to be used for his traveling throughout the state as Grand Master. By 1972, the lodge's membership was at 242 men, a vast increase over 1919, when it had 36 members, and 1931, when membership totaled 105 men.

Georgiana Davis Masonic Lodge No. 338 today is part of the Free and Accepted Masons of Alabama, with meetings held there the second and fourth Monday of each month.

Cemeteries

The Cahawba Baptist Cemetery, now known to most as the Trussville Cemetery, is likely the most recognizable cemetery in the city. It is located directly across from the Trussville Municipal Building on Main Street. The older side of this cemetery is located near a large magnolia tree on the south end of the cemetery. Potential graves in this area are marked by stones and concrete markers, some of which appear to contain no names or dates, perhaps because they faded over time or were never etched onto stone to begin with. Some of the earliest burials here appear to have taken place in the late 1800s. A historical marker was unveiled at the site on the 140th anniversary of the First Baptist Church of Trussville on July 16, 1961. Thomas K. Truss, Warren Truss and other early settlers of Trussville are buried in this cemetery.

The Mt. Nebo Cemetery is located across the street from Trussville First Presbyterian Church. *Gary Lloyd.*

Mt. Nebo Cemetery is located directly across U.S. Highway 11 from First Presbyterian Church of Trussville. A historical marker that was once located near the church suggests that the cemetery was founded in 1860, seven years before the church was founded. Sinkler Lathem, who deeded plots of land for the church and Georgiana Davis Masonic Lodge No. 338, is buried in this cemetery. Some possible grave sites here are marked only by rocks.

Mount Olive Cemetery sits atop a hill overlooking Interstate 59 and Deerfoot Parkway. This cemetery belonged to the former Mount Olive Church and is now managed by Deerfoot Baptist Church.

The Massey Historical Cemetery is located on the north end of Trussville, near the Advent Circle area off U.S. Highway 11. A historical marker from the Alabama Historical Association placed on the site says that Samuel Massey and his brother-in-law Duke William Glenn first settled the territory in February 1814 with Lieutenant Colonel Reuben Nash's Regiment, South Carolina Volunteer Militia, to help defeat the Creek Indians in the War of 1812. Samuel Massey returned to settle the land where the cemetery now sits months before Alabama became a state on December 14, 1819.

Jefferson Memorial Funeral Home and Gardens is likely one of the largest cemeteries in Jefferson County, located on one hundred acres along U.S. Highway 11 across from the Colonial Promenade at Tutwiler Farm shopping center in the city of Birmingham, though most Trussville residents handle their funeral needs here. Jefferson Memorial was established in 1949, and the cemetery is sectioned off for veterans and their spouses, Masons and babies. The Old Rugged Cross section is an Easter Sunday sunrise service is held each year. The ten-thousand-square-foot funeral home was built in 1985 and includes a chapel with a private family entrance and seating area. A sanctuary inside seats about three hundred people, and the building also includes two parlors, two large lobby areas and a coffee room. Jefferson Memorial Funeral Home and Gardens serves an average of 650 families per year.

Trussville Public Library

Not long after the Cahaba Project opened in April 1938, area residents expressed an interest in starting a library to be run by a volunteer librarian. Jean Glenn was the first volunteer. The library was moved several times in its formative years, from the first high school to the Cahaba management office,

The Trussville Public Library, located in the Cahaba Project, is one of the most popular public libraries in Jefferson County. *Gary Lloyd.*

to what is now Heritage Hall from 1948 to 1964 and, finally, to its present location on Parkway Drive beside the John C. Yarbrough Community Center. In a December 1964 report titled "Operation Library," the Trussville Library Board outlined its plan for a new library building on Parkway Drive, saying that the entire Trussville area would "be a better place in which to live when this well-planned modern library is completed, for through its inviting doors will come vast numbers of people from toddlers to retired citizens, like generations before them, to pursue the kind of purposeful activity a good library affords."

The first library building was dedicated in 1965 by then mayor John Yarbrough and Librarian Nettie Lightsey. Other librarians have been Mrs. T.A. Cox, Mrs. G.D. Lightsey, Mrs. Claude Parkel, Mrs. Gray Hanlin, Mrs. Sam Tate, Mrs. Peeples, Mrs. Janet Rose Lyons, Mrs. Joyce Willis, Mrs. Brenda Brasher, Valerie Holmes Baker and Emily Tish. The library has grown from needing one volunteer to a staff of fourteen paid employees.

The library in 1978 joined the Jefferson County Library Cooperative and added an automated computer system. In 1988, it underwent a substantial renovation when it added a children's room. In 1996, the library was temporarily relocated to two classrooms in the John C. Yarbrough Community Center while another major renovation took place. That renovation entailed a remodeling of the existing structure and an addition that doubled the library's size. The newly renovated library opened in November 1997 and was dedicated on May 17, 1998. The library today is at capacity, and there are plans to expand it into the community center next door in the future. In 2013, the Trussville Public Library registered more than twenty thousand visits per month and circulated between thirty thousand and forty thousand items per month, making it one of the most productive public libraries in Jefferson County.

Chapter 10

TRUSSVILLE BOOMS

The growth in population in Trussville between 1970 and 1980 is relatively insignificant. A population of 2,984 in 1970 grew to 3,507 in 1980, an increase of 17.5 percent. But in the 1980s, a boom began in Trussville, a boom that has continued since that time. Trussville still had its two traffic lights like it did in the 1970s, but a series of annexations and future plans for commercial growth deemed the city as progressive in the 1980s.

Between the spring of 1985 and the fall of 1986, Trussville's land area roughly tripled. In that time period, the city approved petitions for about three hundred landowners to become part of the city. Already a rapidly growing city, Trussville grew even more quickly from the frenzy of annexations. "I would love to see Trussville stay the way it was," then mayor Charles Grover said. "But those days are gone. All we can do now is try to control the growth."

In May 1986, the Trussville City Council rezoned seventy-three acres off U.S. Highway 11 for the purpose of a two-hundred-home subdivision, office building and small shopping center. The neighborhood was and still is Calumet Downs, a popular subdivision in Trussville. The next month, the Trussville City Council annexed the Cahaba Valley Golf and Country Club, now known as Trussville Country Club, near the St. Clair County line.

Considering Trussville's location just outside the city of Birmingham and at the intersection of Interstate 59 and Interstate 459, controlling the growth was a difficult task. By 1990, the city's population had grown to 8,044 people, a 129 percent increase over the 3,507 people at the time of the

1980 U.S. census. Good schools and affordable land a decent distance from the hustle and bustle of a big city and the convenience of interstate travel aided in Trussville's growth.

The early to mid-1990s were significant for the city of Trussville relative to commercialization. With residential growth came plans for necessary commercial developments. In December 1994, the Trussville City Council voted to adopt the U.S. 11 Corridor Plan, hailed by city officials at the time as a milestone in urban design and planning. Proponents of the plan said that it would prevent rapid, uncontrolled growth from making U.S. Highway 11 look like a cluttered stretch of businesses. Critics, including commercial developers, believed that the plan came with too much regulation and would halt needed development in the area.

In late 1995, Deerfoot Parkway, a 3.2-mile stretch of roadway from U.S. Highway 11 to Old Springville Road in Clay, opened. About 1,950 acres of undeveloped land had been at the center of the city's and developers' attention for more than a decade. Deerfoot Parkway connects to Interstate 59 and also spans a section of the Cahaba River. Today, much of the land accompanying this roadway is undeveloped, especially on the side closest to U.S. Highway 11. There are, however, some subdivisions and churches.

According to a city of Trussville residential growth report from 1996, between 1980 and September 1996, eight of sixty-two reported subdivisions had all their lots completed. Of the sixty-two residential subdivisions, there were twenty-nine, including the eight at full capacity, that had 75 percent or more of their lots completed. Popular subdivisions Carrington Lakes, Hidden Trace, Lexington Oaks, Maplewood, Old Mill Run, Pepper Tree and Pilgrims Rest were all at a 35 percent completion rate or lower in September 1996, leaving plenty of room for residential growth in the city.

What in part helped to attract families to fill these lots were likely two of the most significant commercial developments in the city of Trussville's history. In June 1998, the Trussville City Council annexed nearly eight hundred acres of land on both sides of Chalkville Mountain Road for the purpose of a shopping center to be called Trussville Crossings. The main commercial attractions that came to Trussville as part of the development were a Walmart SuperCenter and a sixteen-screen Regal Cinema. At the time of construction, the city was garnering about $2.5 million in sales tax revenue. Mayor Gene Melton predicted in 1998 that the new shopping center itself would generate $2 million in sales tax revenue. Some stores were expected to be finished by Christmas 1999, but most opened in the spring of 2000. The Trussville Crossings shopping area today includes

Walmart, Regal Cinema, Buffalo Wild Wings, Hibbett Sports, Big Lots, Bath and Body Works, Marshalls, Hallmark, Milo's, Chick-fil-A, What-A-Burger, Sam's Club, Kohl's, Pet Smart, Konomi, Moe's Southwest Grill, Zaxby's and other shops and restaurants.

Just thirteen months after the Trussville City Council annexed the Chalkville Mountain Road property for Trussville Crossings, it voted five to one in August 1999 to allow the mayor to negotiate a deal with Colonial Properties Trust to develop a shopping center on U.S. Highway 11 at the former TGA golf driving range property. Colonial wanted the city's help with roads and other infrastructure requirements and asked for up to $975,000.00. The city council two months later approved of Mayor Gene Melton signing a $975,000.00 contract with Colonial Properties Trust for the sixty-acre shopping center. The contract stipulated that the city would reimburse Colonial Properties Trust for some infrastructure expenses through tax revenue once the retail stores opened. Once the shopping center, called Colonial Promenade at Tutwiler Farm, opened, the developer was to receive $0.75 for every $1.00 of retail tax revenue until the $975,000.00 was paid off. Once that figure was paid off, city officials at the time predicted an additional $3 million to $4 million in tax revenue per year. The two anchor stores at the shopping center, the Home Depot and SuperTarget, opened in the fall of 2000. The Home Depot opened on September 28, 2000, and SuperTarget held its grand opening on October 8, 2000. Other notable stores that opened included Books-A-Million, Bed Bath & Beyond, T.J. Maxx, Michaels, Old Navy and Academy Sports & Outdoors. These stores and others still anchor the U.S. Highway 11 shopping area in Trussville.

In 2000, the U.S. census reported that Trussville had a population of 12,924 people, split almost evenly between males and females. The population at the new millennium was an increase of nearly 61 percent over the city's population in 1990. With a growing population and money on hand, the City of Trussville broke away from the Jefferson County School System and formed its own school system in 2004. The Hewitt-Trussville High School class of 2006 was the last to graduate as part of the Jefferson County School System.

With budding shopping opportunities, a new school system and growing neighborhoods, the progressive city with an old-town feel in 2005 was ranked by *Money* magazine as the fifty-sixth-best place to live in the United States. The report noted that Trussville's median household income was $62,425 and median home price was $182,826. The one hundred best places' average for 2005 was a median household income of $68,053 and a median home price of $315,351, proving Trussville to be an up-and-coming yet affordable city in which to live. In the report's quality-of-life category, it noted Trussville's personal crime risk was a 26, with the best places to live averaging a 69 and the national average being 100. Trussville carried a 38 on property crime risk, with the best places averaging a 78 and the national average being 100. The lower the number, the better the quality of life, something Trussville officials continue to promote. The report included more than 1,300 cities with populations greater than fourteen thousand with above-average income, population growth and real estate appreciation during the previous five years.

In October 2006, Trussville added more to its commercial base when the Pinnacle at Tutwiler Farm opened behind the Colonial Promenade at Tutwiler Farm, visible from Interstate 59. The $100 million shopping center was developed by Colonial Properties Trust and is anchored by two Belk stores and JCPenney. Other popular stores include hhgregg, Best Buy, Aéropostale, American Eagle, Bama Fever/Tiger Pride, Buckle, Chico's, Foot Locker, Kay Jewelers, Haverty's, Kirkland's Home, Lane Bryant, Lenscrafters, Maurices, New York & Company, Weight Watchers, Wet Seal and Zales Jewelers. Restaurants there include Cajun Steamer, Five Guys Burgers & Fries, La Bamba Mexican Cantina Grill, Logan's Roadhouse, Red Robin and Rock 'N' Roll Sushi.

The additions of well-known retail stores and restaurants has proven successful for Trussville. The city received $13.43 million in sales tax revenue for the 2006–07 fiscal year. That number decreased to $12.77 million for the 2007–08 fiscal year due to a huge downturn in the national economy. The city earned $11.91 million in sales tax for the 2010–11 fiscal year, when the economy was still facing a tough struggle. The 2010 population in Trussville had grown to 19,933 people.

The Trussville City Council in September 2011 voted to increase the city's sales tax by $0.01 to $0.10, citing capital improvements such as an expansion at the Trussville Public Library, downtown revitalization and road extensions as projects necessary for the city. As a result, Trussville garnered $17.39 million in sales tax in 2012. In August 2013, city officials said that the sales tax growth for that year was flat compared with 2012.

In March 2013, the city reached a fairly significant milestone when it opened a compressed natural gas pump at the Chevron station on Deerfoot Parkway. The CNG fueling station was the result of a public-private partnership in which the Trussville Utilities Board loaned McCullough Oil $1.08 million for the project, a total to be repaid with part of the proceeds of

CNG sales. The cost of CNG in early 2013 was $1.55 per gallon, compared to about $3.20 for regular unleaded gasoline. Using CNG is important to Mayor Gene Melton, who said about forty city vehicles, including Trussville Police Department Chevrolet Tahoes and city dump trucks, run on CNG. Melton eventually wants all city vehicles to run on CNG. Melton pushes CNG to other municipalities and has spoken about it to classes at Auburn University, saying that it is a domestic fuel source that burns cleaner than traditional gasoline. Vehicles that run on CNG can accumulate up to fifteen thousand miles between oil changes and require less maintenance than traditional fuel-burning vehicles, Melton said. When the Trussville CNG fueling station opened, it became one of just four other cities in the state with one. Others are in Birmingham, Tuscaloosa, Pell City and Evergreen.

The Trussville Planning and Zoning Board in October 2013 approved a new downtown master plan for the city, recommending that the Trussville City Council amend the city's zoning ordinance for downtown development and amend the city's sign ordinance to include regulations for the downtown district. Implementation of those plans meant, over the course of likely a decade or longer, that Trussville would need to have flood mitigation projects, traffic and streetscape improvements, a public shared parking system, business support and recruitment and downtown zoning and design standards. The Trussville City Council adopted the downtown master plan in December 2013.

On October 22, 2013, the Trussville City Council took its first big step toward implementing the plan when it approved a memorandum of understanding between itself and Ellison Investments LLC for the purchase of 1,839 square feet of property on North Chalkville Road near Main Street. The city acquired the property for $250,000. That property, along with other adjoining properties, including Braden's Furniture, are located where the city is set to construct a dedicated right turn lane from North Chalkville Road to Main Street. The city acquired a former dentist's office building on the corner of North Chalkville Road and Linden Street for $370,000 in December 2013.

By the end of 2013, the city of Trussville was one of the most rapidly growing cities in Jefferson County. New home construction was on the rise, as evidenced by 121 issued building permits from January 2013 through July 2013. The city issued 125 residential building permits in 2012 alone. In the five-year period from 2003 to 2007, Trussville issued a total of 1,771 residential building permits. From 2008 to 2012, when the national economy was at its worst since the Great Depression, Trussville issued just 410 residential building permits.

The marker outside the Trussville Municipal Building includes a poem by Everette E. Jones Sr. that he wrote around 1962, in which he calls Trussville the "Gateway to Happy Living." *Gary Lloyd.*

Trussville City Schools in 2013 was having one of its best years in terms of enrollment and student success, the city itself was the commercial hub for the northeastern Jefferson County area and the city's historic Cahaba Project was thriving with homeowners and residents exercising and recreating in the area.

Trussville is not the small bedroom community it once was. It is not considered one of the state's largest cities, either, though the population today does exceed twenty thousand people. It is a combination of the two. It is a close-knit community with various opportunities for shopping, dining and recreation. It is a city that can fulfill all of its citizens' daily needs but also provide them with a glimpse into the past with the Cahaba Project, a snapshot of how simple and quaint life was in the late 1930s. That is what makes the city of Trussville unique and makes it a destination for young families and those just looking to settle somewhere nice. Trussville has something for everyone, and that is why the city has long adopted the moniker, the "Gateway to Happy Living."

BIBLIOGRAPHY

Alabama High School Football Historical Society. Hewitt-Trussville football search. ahsfhs.org.

"All About Trussville." Booklet, 1989.

Bailey, Tom. "Trussville Loses Part of Self as Old School Burns." *Birmingham News*, May 11, 1973.

Billingsley, Ann Bradford. *The First Fifty Years: A History of the Trussville Southside Baptist Church*. Booklet, July 1991.

Birmingham News, August 11, 1976.

———. "Sinkhole Work Costs Schools $70,000." August 30, 2000.

———. "Trussville's Schools at Top of Class in Winning National Awards." June 6, 1990.

———. "Trussville Tax Bill Gets Senate Approval." April 16, 2004.

Boles, J.W. "Real Past Is Trussville's Boast." *Birmingham News-Age Herald*, Sunday, December 30, 1928.

Bolton, Mike. "H-T Athletic Complex Construction to Begin." *Birmingham News*, April 30, 1985.

———. "Trussville Changing, but Some Not Happy about 'Progress.'" *Birmingham News*, June 20, 1985.

Bouma, Katherine, "Gold Kist Fined for Polluting Cahaba Again." *Birmingham News*, March 2, 2001.

Bradford, Paul E., and Ray W. Owens. "105 Years of Freemasonry: History of Georgiana Davis Lodge No. 338, Trussville, Alabama, 1867–1972." Trussville, AL: Georgiana Davis Lodge No. 338, 1972.

Buttram, Scott. "The Basement Founder Matt Pitt Charged Again." *Trussville Tribune*, August 22, 2013.

Cahaba Community Association. Executive board minutes, March 9, 1944.
———. Meeting minutes, July 1946.
———. Meeting minutes, August 22, 1946.
———. Meeting minutes, August 30, 1946.
———. Meeting minutes, October 8, 1946.
———. Meeting minutes, November 7, 1946.
———. Meeting minutes, April 8, 1947.
———. Meeting minutes, May 28, 1947.
Caldwell, Carla. "East Jeffco Students Face Big Changes." *Birmingham News*, April 29, 1993.
———. "Report Says Trussville Could Support System; Non-Resident Students May Stay." *Birmingham News*, March 4, 1992.
———. "School Board Isn't Quite Ready to Call It Quits." *Birmingham News*, October 22, 1992.
———. "Trussville Gives $250,000 toward Land Purchase for Area Overpass." *Birmingham News*, August 31, 1992.
———. "Trussville Officials Get More Questions." *Birmingham News*, March 2, 1992.
———. "Trussville Process Bypasses Public." *Birmingham News*, April 30, 1992.
———. "Trussville School Debate Continues." *Birmingham News*, December 18, 1991.
Chapman, Michaelle. "Group Opposes Establishing Trussville City School System." *Birmingham News*, February 12, 1992.
Cronkite, Sue, "Clay-Trussville High School Takes on Fortress-Like Design." *Birmingham News*, August 31, 1980.
———. "Trussville Looking Forward to Progressive Year in 1981." *Birmingham News*, January 1, 1981.
Crowson, Bryan. "Council OK of U.S. 11 Corridor Plan Hailed as 'Milestone' in Urban Design." *Birmingham News*, December 15, 1994.
———. "Council Vote Annexes Maplewood." *Birmingham News*, March 16, 1995.
———. "Gold Kist Fined $19,000 for Waste." *Birmingham News*, October 27, 1993.
———. "Mayor Honored for Years of Service." *Birmingham News*, May 1996.
———. "Opening of Clay-Chalkville High Will Give Hewitt-Trussville Breathing Room." *Birmingham News*, January 29, 1996.
———. "Sports Complex Eyes Opener by '94." *Birmingham News*, December 15, 1993.
———. "Steering Committee Works to Get Stadium." *Birmingham News*, September 6, 1995.
———. "Teachers Credited for Blue Ribbon." *Birmingham News*, July 9, 1993.

Davis, John. "Lack of Land Delays Schools." *Birmingham News*, December 8, 1993.

Debro, Anita, "Architect Chosen for New Trussville High School." *Birmingham News*, July 27, 2005.

———. "Board Faces Increase in Cost of New High School." *Birmingham News*, October 12, 2005.

———. "Board Plans Tax-Built High School." *Birmingham News*, December 15, 2004.

———. "Capital Plan Includes New High School." *Birmingham News*, February 16, 2005.

———. "City Must Add $132,600 to Widen U.S. 11 at Schools." *Birmingham News*, July 31, 2002.

———. "Contract OK'd for City's First School System Superintendent." *Birmingham News*, October 12, 2004.

———. "Form School System by '04, Consultant Tells Trussville." *Birmingham N*ews, May 3, 2002.

———. "Repairs Raise Tab for School Projects." *Birmingham News*, November 22, 2002.

———. "Sales Tax Hike Gets Mixed Response." *Birmingham News*, January 10, 2002.

———. "School Board Approved; Seats Filled." *Birmingham News*, May 26, 2004.

———. "School to Close Doors in '03." *Birmingham News*, December 19, 2001.

———. "Separate System Eyed by Fall, 2005." *Birmingham News*, February 25, 2004.

———. "Three School Chief Finalists Named." *Birmingham News*, August 26, 2004.

———. "Trussville, Jeffco Work Out Plans for New School System." *Birmingham News*, March 15, 2005.

———. "Trussville to Boost Sales Tax to 8 Cents." *Birmingham News*, January 25, 2002.

Doster Construction HTHS project portfolio. dosterconstruction.com.

Federal Public Housing Authority. "Report on the Proposed Incorporated Town of Trussville." Letter, March 11, 1947.

First Baptist Church. 140th Anniversary Booklet, 1821–1961. Trussville, AL, July 16, 1961.

First United Methodist Church. "History of the First United Methodist Church, Trussville, Alabama, 1869–1969." Trussville, AL, n.d.

Foss, Sara. "Amerex Head Breaks New Ground for School." *Birmingham Post-Herald*, August 7, 2001.

Frieden, Kitty, "Doss Favors Trussville Site." *Birmingham News*, April 10, 1979.

Girl Scouts of North-Central Alabama. Board of Directors Minutes, May 9, 2012.

Gorman, Gene, "Sinkhole by Junior High Forces Issue." *Birmingham News*, February 10, 1999.

———. "Sinkhole Swallows City's Dollars." *Birmingham News*, May 21, 1999.

———. "'Sleeping Giant' of Trussville Ready to Boom." *Birmingham News*, June 6, 1998.

Hamilton, Francis Dew. "A Firm Foundation." N.p., July 14, 1821–July 14, 1996.

Hickerson, Patrick. "Colonial Properties Contracted for Trussville Shopping Center." *Birmingham News*, October 14, 1999.

———. "Hewitt Elementary's Size Inspires New Construction." *Birmingham News*, November 8, 2000.

———. "Mayor Opposes Gold Kist Permit." *Birmingham News*, November 1, 2000.

———. "New Trussville Stores to Open." *Birmingham News*, September 6, 2000.

———. "Offer Made to Help Pay for School." *Birmingham News*, February 14, 2001.

———. "Trussville to Get Two New Schools." *Birmingham News*, April 17, 2001.

———. "Two New Schools Planned for Trussville." *Birmingham News*, April 3, 2001.

Hicks, Roderick. "Walsh Set to Give Back Trussville School's Name." *Birmingham Post-Herald*, October 7, 1987.

Ingram, Charlie. "Trussville Extends Its Reach into St. Clair by Annexing Golf, Country Club at Meet." *Birmingham News*, June 3, 1986.

———. "Trussville Growth Boasts Problems/Opportunities," *Birmingham News*, November 6, 1986.

Jacobson, Jayna, and Ann Harvey. "Trussville Mayor Suffers Fatal Attack at Council Meeting." *Birmingham News*, July 20, 1982.

Jones, Melanie. "Education Officials 'Still Open' to Suggestions for School Site." *Birmingham News*, August 12, 1980.

———. "Jefferson Board Approves Purchase of Land for New High School; Ends Three-Year Wait." *Birmingham News*, January 23, 1981.

———. "New Homes Clear Hurdle in Trussville." *Birmingham News*, May 15, 1986.

Jones, Melanie, and Bryan Crowson. "Two New Jefferson County Schools Mean District Line Changes Coming." *Birmingham News*, May 5, 1993.

Knox, David. "City Hopes to Get Trendy Shops." *Birmingham News*, September 1, 1999.

Lloyd, Gary, "Age Lowered for Trussville Senior Center Participation." *Trussville Tribune*, July 4, 2013.

———. "Blalock Building Company Approved to Build New Trussville Stadium." *Trussville Tribune*, July 8, 2013.

———. "Camp Coleman Now to Be Rested Friday, Not Closed." *Trussville Tribune*, May 29, 2013.

———. "Camp Coleman Property Plan Reconsidered." *Trussville Tribune*, June 12, 2013.

———. "Matt Pitt's Probation Revoked, Will Serve Remainder of Yearlong Sentence." *Trussville Tribune*, October 17, 2013.

———. "Redevelopment Authority Approves Final Lease Negotiations for Former Food World." *Trussville Tribune*, July 18, 2013.

———. "School Board Gives Neill 'Outstanding' Evaluation for First Year." *Trussville Tribune*, August 8, 2013.

———. "Skating Rink Owner Remembered as Dedicated, Independent." *Trussville Tribune*, March 21, 2013.

———. "Stop Signs to Be Removed from Camp Coleman Entrance." *Trussville Tribune*, July 24, 2013.

———. "Trussville Authorizes Closing on Property for Right Turn Lane, Will Cost $250,000." *Trussville Tribune*, October 31, 2013.

———. "Trussville City Council Honors Ned Paine." *Trussville Tribune*, April 24, 2013.

———. "Trussville CNG Pump Opens." *Trussville Tribune*, March 19, 2013.

———. "Trussville Industrial Board Wants Properties Online 'Quick.'" *Trussville Tribune*, October 11, 2013.

———. "Trussville OKs First Step to Acquire Property for N. Chalkville Right Turn." *Trussville Tribune*, October 24, 2013.

———. "Trussville P&Z Approves Downtown Master Plan." *Trussville Tribune*, October 17, 2013.

———. "Trussville Sales Tax Growth Flat Compared with 2012." *Trussville Tribune*, August 8, 2013.

———. "Trussville to Install Security Fence at Former Gold Kist." *Trussville Tribune*, March 28, 2013.

Massey, Carol, and Earl Massey. *Trussville through the Years*. 2nd printing. Tarrant, AL: Valley Printing Company, 1988.

Oliver, Mike. "Bush Visits, Urges Voters to Join Team." *Birmingham News*, July 20, 1986.

Parrish, Joni. Interview with the author, July 8, 2013.

Pierce, Phil. "Some Don't Want Middle School Named for Burkett." *Birmingham News*, October 5, 1987.

Place, Patsy, and Dave White. "Border Battle Steps Up; Mayor Fights Back." *Birmingham News*, May 27, 1985.

Poe, Ryan. "Gun Maker Buys Bessemer Buildings for $1.37M." *Birmingham Business Journal*, September 26, 2013.

Purcell, Douglas Clare. *The Making of a City: Trussville, Alabama, 1820–1970*. Booklet, August 17, 1970.

Seale, Kathy. "Amerex to Donate Land for New School." *Birmingham News*, July 28, 1999.

Singleton, William C., III. "Freeman Picked by Trussville." *Birmingham News Post-Herald*, August 31, 2004.

"Swimming Pool to Open June 2nd," *Trussville Advertiser*, May 29, 1956.

Thornton, William. "Trussville Board of Education Approves Contract Settlement with Suzanne Freeman." *Birmingham News*, July 16, 2012.

———. "Trussville Taps Samford Professor Pattie Neill as Interim Superintendent." *Birmingham News*, July 20, 2012.

Trussville Advertiser. "Hey, Kids! The Pool Opens Tomorrow." June 1, 1955.

———. "James Barr Offers for Mayor's Post." September 5, 1960.

"Trussville cemeteries" search. interment.com.

Trussville Times. "John C. Yarbrough Files For Mayor in City Election." June 24, 1964.

White, Dave. "Some of City's Plans to Annex Fire Up a Fight." *Birmingham News*, May 24, 1985.

Woodward, Joseph H., II. *Alabama Blast Furnaces*. Tuscaloosa: University of Alabama Press, 2007, 145–46.

Websites

www.amerex-fire.com
www.bobsmithconstruction.com
www.bradenfurniture.com
www.cafeonmainfood.com
www.clearbranch.org
www.crosspointchurch.info
www.deerfootbaptist.org
www.deerfootcbc.org
www.epct.org
www.fcftrussville.com
www.girlscoutsnca.org
www.hiopcc.org
www.jmgardens.com
www.joelsrestaurant.net
www.mcphersonoil.com
www.mtjoybaptist.com
www.rbconline.net
www.stjosephtrussville.org
www.trussvillechurchofchrist.com
www.trussvillelibrary.com

INDEX

ABOUT THE AUTHOR

Gary Lloyd, a Trussville, Alabama native, has been the editor of the *Trussville Tribune* from November 2010 to June 2012 and January 2013 to the writing of this book. Lloyd has also been a general assignment reporter for the *Magee (MS) Courier/Simpson County News*; an associate editor at Cahaba Media Group in Birmingham, Alabama; and a freelancer for the *Tuscaloosa News* and the *Birmingham News*. Lloyd earned his bachelor's degree in journalism from the University of Alabama in December 2009, minoring in American studies. He graduated from Hewitt-Trussville High School in 2006.